# Beautiful Bonds

## A Celebration of Women and Friendship

LATONYA STERLING

Beautiful Bonds
A Celebration of Women and Friendship
By Latonya Sterling

Unless otherwise noted, all Scripture quotations are taken from the *Holy Bible, New International Version*®, NIV®. Copyright ©1973, 1978, 1984, 2011 by Biblica, Inc.™ Used by permission. All rights reserved worldwide.

ISBN: 9798999589712

First Edition

Cover design generated ChatGPT

Published by Latonya LSimmons Sterling

Contact: latonyasterling@gmail.com

Printed in the United States of America

*Latonya L. Sterling*

# Dedication

*To every woman who has ever spoken life into me,*
*stood beside me, challenged me to grow, or simply loved*
*me as I am—this book is for you.*
*You are the beautiful bonds that have shaped my journey.*
*I am forever grateful for my sisters, friends, mentors, family,*
*and co-laborers who have left an imprint on my heart.*
*Thank you for showing me what real, authentic*
*sisterhood looks like.*

*With Love,*
*Latonya*

*Proverbs 27:17 (NIV)*

*"As iron sharpens iron, so one*

*person sharpens another."*

### *A Prayer of Gratitude for Beautiful Bonds*

*Father God,*

*I come before You with a heart overflowing with gratitude for the beautiful women You have placed in my life. Thank You for every sister, friend, mentor, and mother-figure who has loved me with Your love. Thank You for their prayers that lifted me when I was weak, their words of encouragement that gave me hope, and their gentle correction that helped me stay on the right path.*

*Lord, I'm so thankful for the women who have walked with me through seasons of joy and sorrow, who have celebrated my victories and held me up in my struggles. You have surrounded me with women who have sharpened me, challenged me, and helped me grow into who You've called me to be. Their kindness, patience, and faithfulness have been a reflection of Your heart toward me.*

*Thank You for the bonds that go beyond titles, beyond circumstances, and beyond time—bonds that are rooted in Your love and truth. Help me to never take these relationships for granted. Help me to be that same kind of friend to others—a vessel of Your grace, encouragement, and love.*

*I give You all the glory, Lord, for the gift of sisterhood, for You are the Author of every beautiful bond in my life.*

*In Jesus' Name,*
*Amen.*

# Table of Contents

# Introduction

# A Different Story

Too often, some women have been taught to see other women as rivals instead of sisters. I have often heard women say things like, "I don't get along with other women," or "Women are too catty and dramatic." It's a narrative that has followed many of us—a belief that female relationships are complicated, fragile, and filled with drama. But, that hasn't been my story. In fact, my experience has been just the opposite.

From preschool to high school, and into my adult years, I've been surrounded by women who have stood by me, supported me, challenged me, and helped me grow. These friendships have been rich, sincere, and lasting—not because they were perfect, but because they were honest, loving, and full of grace.

This book is my way of celebrating those women and their place in my life. It's a collection of real stories about real friendships—about connection, loyalty, laughter, and sometimes loss. Each woman I share about is not better or more important than the others, but each has added something unique and irreplaceable to my journey. One may have strengthened me with wisdom, while another lifted me with laughter, and another held me steady through prayer. Together, their presence has woven a beautiful tapestry of support, each thread carrying its own worth. It's not about sisters by blood or even race. The women who've walked with me have come from many different backgrounds. This is not a story of sameness. It's a story of unity. These are not sisters by culture or color—but by heart.

The friendships I share in these pages were built across lunch tables, late-night phone calls, shared tears, and spontaneous laughter. I want you, the reader, to walk away knowing that meaningful friendship between women isn't just possible—it's powerful. It's life-giving.

If you've ever felt like deep, lasting friendships with other women were too difficult to find, I hope this book changes your mind. And if you've been blessed, like I have, to experience them—may these stories remind you that you are not alone, and may this book feel like home.

# Chapter *1*
# How True Friendships Are Formed

True friendships are not made overnight. They don't come with instructions, guarantees, or perfect timing. They are built moment by moment, often in the quiet places—across shared meals, in whispered secrets, through tears, laughter, and vulnerability.

Valuable friendships begin when we choose to be present, when we're willing to see and be seen, without needing to be impressive. Sometimes they start with common interests, but they become lasting through commitment, trust, and a willingness to grow alongside one another.

Over the years, I've come to understand that enduring friendships between women aren't built by accident. They are formed through intentionality—choosing to reach out, check in, and be available even when life gets busy. Authentic friendships grow when we learn to truly listen, not to fix or offer quick answers, but to understand and sit with another woman's story, even when it's uncomfortable or unfamiliar. Grace becomes essential in these relationships, as we give each other room to be human—to make mistakes, to have off seasons, and to drift at times, knowing that love remains.

There are times when there is distance in friendships that are necessary or beyond your control. This doesn't mean you are no longer friends. Sometimes life circumstances— like marriage, raising children, career changes, or even relocation—can create space that wasn't there before. Other times, distance is needed for personal growth, healing, or to gain perspective. But, distance doesn't always equal disconnection. Too often, women dissolve friendships over misunderstandings or seasons of silence that could have been repaired with a conversation, patience, or grace. Friendships aren't perfect because they consist of imperfect people, but that's also what makes them so valuable. When we choose to work through the hard moments instead of walking away, we discover the depth, resilience, and beauty that true friendship can hold.

Loyalty is the anchor of these bonds, being the kind of friend who is safe, dependable, and rooted, someone who can be trusted with both joys and struggles. True friendship also celebrates without competition, rejoicing in each other's victories and blessings without the need to compare or compete. And most importantly, real friendships are grounded in truth, where love gives us the courage to speak honestly, but always with compassion. These are the threads that weave lasting, life-giving connections among women, creating friendships that stand the test of time.

Friendship among women can be one of the most beautiful gifts in life. It's a place of strength, tenderness, safety, and spiritual encouragement. It's where we remind one another who we are and whose we are.

In the chapters that follow, you'll meet women who have stood by me in different seasons and played different roles—but each of them helped shape who I am. Some friendships were unexpected. Others were instant. A few were tested. All of them were treasured.

These are the beautiful bonds that have influenced my life, and I invite you to meet the women who made those bonds possible. These are the women who remind me that friendship is not just something we have—it's something we become for one another.

# Chapter *2*

# The First Woman Who Loved Me

*Honoring My Amazing Mom Mary Johnson*

If I'm going to write a book about the amazing women in my life, it only makes sense to begin with the very first woman who ever loved me—my mom, Mary Johnson. She was just 19 years old when she became pregnant with me. At the time, she was already a single mother raising my older brother, who was only one. I'm so grateful to God that she chose to keep me. And I'm just as thankful that God didn't let her walk that journey alone. Before I was even born, He brought a wonderful man into her life—the man who would become my dad. But that's another story.

As far back as I can remember, my mom was always there. Every school program, every event—she showed up. One moment stands out vividly: I was in preschool, standing on stage during a school performance. All the kids were singing, but I stood there crying. Without hesitation, my mom came out of the audience and rescued me from the stage. That's the kind of mom she's always been.

She did it all. She worked outside the home, took us to every doctor's appointment, made sure we had three meals a day, and kept the house clean. She didn't just care for us—she taught us. We knew how to do chores and how to take care of ourselves.

My sister and I were always looking good. Mom did our hair herself. I remember sitting on the floor between her legs in front of the stove as she pressed our hair with a hot comb and that thick blue grease—or sometimes the green one. When she finished, we were cute!

She is so gifted. I remember her upholstering furniture by hand, weaving flower holders out of cord (macrame), making potholders, and crafting beautiful, beaded designs. She taught me how to do it all. Mom was an incredible seamstress. I still remember the red and white dress she made for me—it had ruffles around the collar, sleeves, and hem, and a bow at the neck. It was my absolute favorite. She also made me a pair of perfectly pleated pink pants and my sister a gorgeous ruffled white blouse. My sister didn't like it, but I wore it proudly with my pink pants and felt like I was something special.

In high school, while other girls were paying seamstresses to make their chorus gowns, my mom made mine. She even made my prom dress. That meant everything to me.

And the meals? Unforgettable. No matter how tired she was after work, we had a home-cooked dinner every night. On the rare occasion when she didn't feel like cooking, she'd whip up homemade biscuits and serve them with King syrup. That was a treat. And when it came to baking, nobody could touch her. No box cakes from my mom. Her German chocolate cake, carrot cake and pineapple cake from scratch, and oven-baked banana pudding were legendary.

She didn't run a business, but she could've. She sold a few of her handmade items like potholders and planters, but most of what she did, she did out of love. Despite everything going on in her life, much of which she never shared—she kept going. She was a fighter, a provider, a nurturer, and a protector.

When she left us with babysitters, she packed everything we could possibly need. No one could say my mother mooched off them—she came prepared. And yes, she was a disciplinarian. I'm thankful to God for holding her back the day I set my sister's bed on fire. (Yes, that really happened.)

There were times I thought she was too hard on me, but looking back, I understand she was protecting me—from myself and from people I wasn't mature enough to recognize as dangerous. We had disagreements. There were times when I even questioned whether she really loved me. But, as I grew up in the Lord, I began to see things differently. I realized that her love had always been there—I just couldn't see it through the haze of my own selfishness and misunderstanding.

There are so many things about my mom that deserve to be celebrated. She wasn't just a provider or a caretaker— she was the heartbeat of our home. She was creative, resourceful, strong, and deeply devoted to her family. She carried more than we will ever know, and still she chose to pour out love in every way she could. Her laughter, her wisdom, her discipline, her talents, and yes, her beautiful voice, all combined to shape the woman I am today. Most people don't know that my mom has an amazing singing voice. She was a secret singer.

I lived at home until I was 32. Some say two grown women can't live in the same house, but that wasn't the case for us. I never pulled the "I'm grown" card. It was her house, and I respected her deeply. I was grateful for the roof she provided and the support she offered. When I went to college, she even let me drive her cool Grand Prix with the T-top. That meant the world to me.

All the complaints I had about her when I was younger faded as I got older. I came to understand that everything she did—every restriction, every decision—was always for my good.

I'll never forget when my husband encouraged me to share some painful truths with Mom that I'd carried for years. When I finally opened up, she gave me insight that I had never considered. That conversation changed everything. From that moment on, my mom became my friend.

Today, our relationship is stronger than ever. One of the greatest honors of my life is knowing that my walk with Christ inspired her to seek Him for herself. She once told me, "The reason I turned to Christ is because I watched you." That wasn't me—it was God. I never ministered to her directly. She simply watched from a distance and saw Him in me. Jesus once said, *"A prophet is not without honor except in his own town and in his own home"* (Matthew 13:57, NIV). Jesus was talking about Himself. This wasn't a principle as many believed. My mom honored the change she saw in me—and I'll never forget that.

Now, we talk about the Word of God all the time. Whenever I'm scheduled to teach at church, she's my practice congregation. We talk about everything. Sometimes I'm so candid that I embarrass her, but we laugh a lot. I try to talk to her every day so she knows she's loved and never alone.

Caring for my mom is one of my greatest joys. It's not about paying her back, it's simply what's right. When my dad was diagnosed with pancreatic cancer, I knew I had to be there for both of them. That was a tough time, but she carried herself with grace. I saw her weakness, but I also saw God's strength holding her up. She never gave up on my dad. She stood by him and took amazing care of him until the very end. I was so proud of her.

Now, with Dad gone, she's starting a new chapter. She has her moments—she misses the love of her life after more than 50 years—but I see her blooming. It's like watching a child discover a candy store for the first time. She's stepping into something new, and it's my honor to walk with her into this season of rediscovery.

Mom, you were the first woman who ever loved me. Know that not an ounce of your love was wasted. And now, as a woman myself, I understand just how much that love cost—and how beautiful it truly is.

# Chapter 3

# My Sister, My Friend

*Honoring My Sister Eugenia Harrison*

I have met quite a few women who do not have a good relationship with their sisters. Some carry deep wounds, others long for a closeness that never came, and some simply drift apart with time. I can't really imagine that kind of life, because for me, my sister Gina has always been more than just family—she has been my best friend. From our earliest days to now, our bond has been unshakable, and I thank God for the gift of her presence in my life.

First things first—don't call my sister Eugenia. Doing so might just cost you your life. The funny thing is, she may not even realize that her name actually means well-born, noble, of good lineage—a reflection of dignity and strength. It's a name with weight and beauty, made even more special because it's derived from my dad's name, Eugene. But since she prefers "Gina"—and because I value both my life and our relationship—you'll see me call her that throughout this chapter.

Gina and I are three years apart, but age never put a barrier between us. When we were in elementary school, Gina followed me everywhere. She wanted to be with me so much that sometimes I felt like I couldn't hang out with my friends unless she was right there, too. One day, in frustration, I told her to go away and find her own friends.

She looked so hurt as she walked off, and I felt an emptiness immediately. Within minutes, tears filled my eyes—I had sent away my closest friend. I left my group and went searching for her. I finally spotted her standing in a crowd, watching something, and I walked right over and stood by her side. From that day forward, I never sent Gina away again. I realized she wasn't a bother—she was my friend.

Our childhood was filled with endless games and creative adventures. We made our own paper dolls, complete with clothing. We built little worlds with paper furniture and tiny food pictures cut out from Sears and Montgomery Ward catalogs. My mom dreaded the mess, but it was our joy. Our Aunt Adele had shown us how to make the dolls, and when Gina got mad, her paper doll would go flying across our paper houses to irritate or get back as us. Sometimes it was annoying, and sometimes it was funny.

We curled strips of newspaper around bobby pins and pretended we had long, flowing hair. We made pom-poms out of old papers and cheered for imaginary teams. We set up a "bank" using our dresser as the counter, with a shoe for a toy phone and pretend cash register. And when no one was watching, we jumped on the beds until our hearts pounded. We climbed trees, made mud pies, and lived in a world of fun and imagination. We even played church. As I preached from a religious book, Gina would shout Amen. But, we had to shut our church down because Momma said we were playing with the Lord. Ha! Looking back, I realize those simple joys built the foundation of a lifelong friendship.

My sister possesses an extraordinary drive and determination. Although she left high school early, she refused to let that decision define her future. Rather than settling for a GED, she enrolled in online courses and persevered until she earned her high school diploma. She went on to complete her associate's degree and continued pursuing further studies with the same commitment. For a time, I even helped her by taking some of her classes alongside her, and together we achieved excellence. Though she eventually paused her studies, today she has returned to her educational journey with renewed focus. I could not be more proud of her resilience, her persistence, and her unwavering belief in the value of education.

There has never been a time when Gina and I cut each other off or stopped speaking for more than 24 hours. I wouldn't give her that long to stay mad at me. That was simply never an option. She has always been too special to me. I remember working at Hardee's as a teenager and using my paycheck to help buy her two gowns for her military balls. Seeing her look so beautiful filled me with pride.

Of course, Gina has always had a little wild side. I still remember her sneaking home with a 40-ounce bottle tucked inside her jacket. I thought, *My goodness, I'm older than her, and I don't even drink!* She had her first real boyfriend before I ever did. Gina was more adventurous, more daring, more ready to try new things. Even today, I know she could move across the world with her husband and thrive because she enjoys new experiences. Me? I've always been the one who prefers staying close to what I know. She's bold, I'm cautious—but our differences balance each other out.

Gina is an amazing mother. She has two daughters and two sons, and her love for them is unwavering. Even when they test her patience, she doesn't give up on them. She may come across as tough at times, but behind her firmness is a heart full of love. She simply doesn't want anyone she cares for to hurt or lack what they need.

One of the sweetest seasons of our lives was when we were pregnant at the same time. Our sons were born just a week apart. My Marcel came early as a preemie, while Gina's Blake was full-term and much bigger. For years, my little boy wore Gina's son's hand-me-downs, and I was totally thankful. Gina never bought anything cheap or flimsy, so my son was always dressed well.

I remember when Gina and her family moved away to Mississippi because her husband Ted was stationed there in the military. I hated for my sister to be so far away. But, thank God for technology. We were able to FaceTime, and it felt like she was right here. My best memory was during the time I was pregnant with Justin. My friend's threw me a surprise baby shower, and my sister drove all the way from Mississippi to be there. I could not believe it. I remember hugging her and crying.

Eventually they moved back to Virginia. Later, when her family was transitioning to buy a new home, they lived with my family for nearly ten months. Those were some of the best months of my life. The house was full of laughter, energy, and companionship. Blake and Bree were my boy's consistent playmates, and Gina's cooking filled the kitchen with aromas that made every meal a joy. She is a phenomenal cook, always making sure her family eats well. I learned so many things from her during that season. She introduced my family to asparagus.

We also became walking partners. Our neighborhood loop was a little over three miles, and we walked it at least four days a week. Those walks became our therapy sessions—moments where we laughed, vented, and dreamed together. When Gina finally told me they had found a house, I selfishly hoped the deal would fall through because I didn't want her to move out. That's how much I loved having her close. We were two women in the house getting along well.

Through the years, I have learned so much from Gina—about motherhood, friendship, courage, and perseverance. She has shown me what it looks like to be both strong and loving, both adventurous and grounded. She has taught me that love sometimes looks like toughness, but it is always rooted in care.

Gina is married to a wonderful man named Ted, and together they've built a beautiful family and life. Watching her thrive as a wife is wonderful to watch.

As I reflect on my bond with Gina, I realize how rare and precious it is. I know not every woman has this kind of relationship with her sister. Some carry scars from betrayal or words that can't be taken back. Some have drifted apart after years of silence. My heart aches for them, because I know the treasure of sisterhood.

If I could give any woman advice about her sister, it would be this: remember that no one is perfect. We all have flaws, and we all need grace. If there is a way to reconcile, do it. Some situations may be too broken to repair—of course, if your sister tried to harm you in extreme ways, that's another story. Nevertheless, forgiveness is essential. If there is room for reconciliation, don't wait. Sisters are too precious to lose.

I am grateful beyond words that God gave me Gina—not just as my sister, but as my lifelong friend. My prayer is that every woman would experience this kind of love in her own family, and if she hasn't, that God would bring other women into her life to fill that void. Because truly, there's nothing like having your sister.

# Chapter 4

# Daughters Who Made Me A Mom

*Honoring Jennifer, Victoria, Tanisha & Taylor*

I have the most amazing daughters in the world. Each of them is unique, carrying a distinctive personality that reflects both the beauty and the complexity of womanhood. I remember asking God early on to help me deal with each of them according to their personalities, because I quickly realized I wasn't raising three identical girls—I was shepherding three very different young ladies.

To give some backdrop, I met their father, Marlon Sterling, over twenty-three years ago while serving in ministry. At the time, he was a single father, and later I became his wife and a mother to our daughters. Together, we learned to grow as a family.

**Jennifer** is our oldest daughter. By the time we married, she was over eighteen and living with her beautiful biological mother, Andreina, so I never had the privilege of raising her day-to-day. But even though I didn't help raise her, she still holds a special place in my heart.

What amazes me about Jennifer is her tenacity. She's the kind of woman who, when she's with you, she is all in—loyal, committed, and true. She is good with money, fiercely devoted to her daughters Kaileigh and Tenley, and there's nothing she wouldn't do for them. She's a little edgy, with a wit and sense of humor that I absolutely love. And no one—

absolutely no one—can stand up to Grandma Marcelina the way Jennifer can!

**Victoria**, my second daughter, is full of life. When I first met her as a little girl, she was six or seven years old, and even then, her personality filled the room. She was boisterous, fun, and very emotional—sometimes needing more support than I knew how to give in the early years of parenting. She had the ability to turn dinner into a comedy show, making up songs at the table and filling the house with laughter.

Tori has always been forgiving and free-spirited. She moved out her senior year of high school to chart her own path, later attending Virginia Commonwealth University, where she earned her bachelor's degree. Today, she lives in Richmond, happily exploring life on her own terms. She's still that fun, adventurous girl at heart, but now she's grown into a woman who knows who she is.

**Tanisha** came into our home a little later. She is just a few months older than Taylor, but she didn't live with us until she was about ten years old. By then, adding her into our household was like throwing another ingredient into an already bubbling pot.

Neesh is a fighter—in the best way. She has always been tenacious, determined, and adventurous. If you dropped her in the wilderness, she would find a way to survive. She is resourceful beyond measure. Finding jobs and opportunities came naturally to her, even when others struggled. She is deeply loyal—if Tanisha is your friend, she will stick by you. Neesh is also very gifted. If you teach her something once, she'll learn it and take it to a whole new level. Even when she faces moments where she wants to throw in the towel, her resilience shines through.

Today, she is married to Justin, a mother to my precious granddaughter Amara, and a woman who has learned to harness her strength with wisdom. She's grown from reacting with her fists to pausing long enough to think first—and that growth is something I deeply admire.

**Taylor** was only four years old when I met her, the youngest at the time, and people always thought she was the quiet one. But I quickly learned that Tay wasn't really quiet—she was simply thoughtful. Serious and reflective, she was never one to pretend. If you upset her, she would let you know. If she didn't like you, she wouldn't fake it. Even as a child, Tay was highly intuitive and would intentionally ask questions to catch people in their lies.

Tay was also the one who challenged me the most, probably because we share such similar personalities. She was the last daughter to leave home, and she left with a clear plan for her life. She knew what kind of man she wanted, what kind of future she hoped for, and most importantly, she learned to trust God at an early age.

She entered a CCAP cooking competition in high school and was awarded a four-year scholarship to the Culinary Institute of America in New York—the best culinary school in the country. One might expect her to chase big restaurants and celebrity chefs, but Taylor's heart wasn't about ambition. Her heart was about helping. She ended up in the education system, first teaching kids how to cook healthy, and now serving as an elementary school teacher. She has a deep compassion for children, especially those who are in need.

During her final year of college, Tay met Colton—an amazing young man of God who would become her husband and the father of their twin girls Alara and Analiz. Colton is not only her husband, but the only boyfriend she has ever had. Their relationship is a beautiful testimony of God's faithfulness.

Raising daughters was both a joy and a challenge, and I didn't always get it right. The girls even nicknamed me "Cruella DeVille" behind my back during those early years because I was unnecessarily strict, I enforced chore charts, and stretched their allowance to teach responsibility. At first, it wasn't easy—we had to learn how to live together and respect one another's differences, but in the process we grew together.

One thing I am grateful for is that our home was never filled with drama or constant sisterly battles. From the beginning, I laid down the rule: there would be no fighting among sisters in my house. They may have had disagreements behind closed doors, but they learned to love each other, to forgive, and to find a way forward.

Now, as adult women, my relationship with them has shifted. I no longer stand over them as the "mom in charge." Instead, I get to be their friend. They can come to me for advice or share their lives with me, and I am careful to respect their boundaries. That shift is one of the sweetest parts of motherhood—watching your daughters grow into women you admire.

One of my prayers has always been that God would allow me to live long enough to see my children grow into successful adults—in Christ, in life, and in family. I am grateful that He has answered that prayer with my girls. I love them as if I had given birth to each one myself. I would fight for them. They are truly special to me. I never had to compete with their biological mothers, and the girls learned to love me for who I am. They don't make me feel like anything less than their mother, and that is one of the greatest gifts they could ever give me.

There is something sacred about the bond between a mother and her daughters. It is a relationship that grows, stretches, and transforms over time. First, you are the teacher, the disciplinarian, the one who sets the rules. But as the years pass, you become the cheerleader, the confidant, and the friend.

Sometimes when your children go through challenges, the natural instinct is to step in—to fix the problem and take away the pain. But, I've learned it's far more important to step back and allow God to do the growing in them. That doesn't mean a parent can never help; it means we must discern whether our involvement will be a help or a hindrance. With my daughters, God has shown me how to walk alongside them in their adult lives without stunting their growth. And even now, as grown women, they continue to teach me new lessons about what it means to be a mother.

A mother's love gives her daughters roots to hold them steady and wings to help them fly. And a daughter's love, when it matures, gives her mother the joy of knowing that every sacrifice, every sleepless night, and every prayer was worth it.

I am honored to be their mother, but even more honored to call them my friends.

# Chapter *5*

# A Friendship for a Lifetime

*Honoring Sabrena Harris*

Everyone has that one friend they've known longer than anyone else. For me, that friend is Sabrena Harris—or as I like to stretch her name, *Sabreeeen.* She has been my friend since preschool, and through every season of life, she has remained one of the most constant, joyful presences in my journey.

She even gave me my nickname, "Tonto," like the Lone Ranger's sidekick, and it stuck for years. I don't even remember her calling me by my birth name much. We grew up in the same neighborhood, went to the same schools, and shared more laughs than I can count. Sabreen was adventurous, bold, and always fun. Her laugh is loud, infectious, and unforgettable—if you were anywhere in the room, you couldn't help but join in.

Some of our childhood antics were dangerously fun. Walking to Stuart Elementary meant passing through a beautiful neighborhood where the houses sat on hills. We would ring the doorbells, then roll down the hills as fast as we could, laughing until our sides ached and running off before anyone caught us. One time, though, our rolling went a little too far—one of us ended up in a rosebush full of thorns! We laughed even harder, even while pulling out the prickly reminders of our mischief.

I loved going to Sabreen's house, especially when her family had gatherings. Her home was full of energy and laughter, with her sister Deedra and her brothers Ron and Alfred. I'll admit, I had a bit of a crush on Ron back then—he was a hottie—but he never paid me any attention. Still, being part of Sabreen's family gave me an excuse to be around.

Sabreen was also a trickster, and there was no shame in her tricks. Once, she invited me to church under the pretense of introducing me to "the finest guy ever." Of course, when I got there, it turned out to be a joke just to get me to church. That was Sabreen—mischievous, clever, and always thinking of ways to make life more fun.

When we graduated high school, life took us in different directions. Sabreen went off to Devry and even served in the Army for a season. Distance separated us physically, but it never weakened the bond we shared.

I had the privilege of being close to her during her years as a young mother. Sabreen was intentional about giving her children experiences—taking them to the zoo, museums, and adventures that enriched their lives. She wasn't a self-absorbed mom; her focus was always on making life better for her children. I often tagged along, and watching her raise her kids blessed me deeply.

One of the most meaningful aspects of our friendship was how it intersected with my walk with God. When I rededicated my life to the Lord, Sabreen respected my new lifestyle. She included me in activities that were good for me and shielded me from those that weren't. She never pressured me to compromise.

I'll never forget the day she came to church, walked to the altar, and gave her heart to Jesus. In our church, anyone who came forward was given a little brown package with a Bible in it. When Sabreen came up to me holding that package, my heart leapt with joy. She told me one of the things she appreciated was that I never preached at her—I just lived my life. My example made her want Jesus for herself. That moment was one of the greatest joys of my spiritual journey.

Over the years, Sabreen has grown into a remarkable woman—educated, accomplished, and always striving to be her best. But her ambition has never been selfish. She cheers others on, celebrating their success as if it were her own.

When it came time for me to get married, it was only proper that Sabreen stood beside me as one of my bridesmaids. There was absolutely no way I could have such an important day without including such an amazing, wonderful friend. Interestingly enough, Sabreen is very tall—and wouldn't you know, one of the groomsmen was also tall—so she ended up perfectly paired!

Eventually, she married a wonderful man named Hezron, and I was honored to stand as a bridesmaid in her wedding, too. What touched me most was when she asked me to be the one to pray for her before she walked down the aisle. Of all the women she could have chosen, she asked me. That moment is still one of the greatest honors of my life.

Sabreen has always managed her friendships well. She has many close friends, and yet somehow, she makes each of us feel like we're her "best friend" in a unique way. She is authentic, intentional, and thoughtful. Even as a young woman, she challenged me to be better. Once, after I cursed in front of her, she simply asked, "Was that really necessary? Couldn't you have found different words?" It hit me. That simple question changed me, curbing my language and keeping me from going down a path of habitual profanity.

I have watched Sabreeen walk through challenging seasons as both a wife and a mother, and I have seen her rise with dignity every time. She faced difficulties that could have broken her spirit, yet she carried herself with remarkable grace. Quitting and failing were never in her vocabulary; instead, she met every challenge with courage, determination, and faith. Her perseverance has been a testament to the strength of her character and the depth of her trust in God. Sabreeen's life is a living example of resilience—an inspiration not only to me, but to everyone who has the privilege of witnessing her journey.

Sabreen is a wonderful friend, wife, and mother. She is loyal, fun, wise, and authentic. I value her deeply and thank God for her presence in my life. Despite the years, time, and distance, there has never been a gap in our friendship.

Childhood friends hold a special place in our hearts. They knew us before life got complicated, before we wore masks, before we had titles and responsibilities. They remind us of who we were, and they anchor us to our beginnings. A true childhood friend carries your history, celebrates your present, and walks with you into your future.

I am grateful that Sabreen is that friend for me. Sabreeeeen isn't just my childhood companion—she's a lifelong sister of the heart.

# Chapter 6

# A Safe Place

*Honoring Ma Patricia Battle*

Have you ever lived in a neighborhood where there was a "neighborhood mom"? Someone who wasn't your biological mother, but who loved, guided, and looked out for all the kids as if they were her own? For me, that person was Patricia Battle—better known to me as Ma. I never even realized she lived in the neighborhood until a new family moved into the house next door to her. I quickly became friends with their kids, Petrina and Shawn, and through spending time at their house, I was introduced to Ma.

Ma lived in the house next to the big open field and the cherry tree we used to climb, picking cherries right off the branches and eating them fresh. But, beyond the cherries, kids just gravitated to her house. I don't know what being at her house meant to anyone else, but for me her home was a safe place where I could vent, cry, complain, or laugh. With Ma, there was no judgment—just honesty. She was a straight shooter, no chaser. She would give you the truth with a side of humor, laughing while she said it, but still making sure you heard what you needed to hear.

Looking back, I realize how important that was for me during the times I was working through difficulties at home. Ma and her husband at the time, Pa, became my neighborhood parents. They always made me feel welcome and treated me like a daughter.

I'll never forget my first getaway with them. Ma and Pa took me to Nags Head one fall on a family trip. The crisp air, the sound of the waves, the beauty of the season—all of it felt magical. More than that, it felt like being part of something steady and whole … a family.

Some of my favorite memories are of sitting on their porch with them and their adult friends. I would just sit, listening to their conversations, their laughter, and their wisdom. It was like sitting in the midst of something bigger than me, soaking up lessons about life just by being near.

As I grew older, Ma's role in my life shifted, but her influence remained just as strong. When she worked at Sentara Norfolk General, she gave me a job as a receptionist. I loved it. I'll never forget the day I accidentally slipped up and called her "Ma" at work. She quickly corrected me: "I'm not Ma at work." She meant it too. I didn't get special treatment. I had to work just as hard as everyone else. But I didn't mind, because I loved being around her. I even quit my second job just so I could spend more time working alongside Ma.

When the office eventually closed down, I was disappointed—not just because I lost the job, but because I lost those daily moments of seeing her. Still, I was grateful that she lived in the neighborhood, and I could always stop by.

Like many relationships in life, time and distance created some space between us. But people like Ma are unforgettable. You can't get rid of them, even if you tried. They become a part of the fabric of who you are.

One of the blessings of Facebook has been the ability to keep up with people who mean so much, even when life takes you in different directions. That's how I've managed to stay in touch with Ma through the years.

The last time I saw her was at my father's Celebration of Life service. It had been a while, but the moment I hugged her, it felt like no time had passed. The same warmth, the same love, the same encouragement was still there.

I'll never forget how much of an encouragement Ma was to me when I needed it most. She stood in the gap at times when I needed a mother figure outside of my home. She was an anchor, a safe harbor, and a source of laughter and wisdom.

Neighborhood moms like Ma are treasures. They are the ones who remind us that love isn't limited by bloodlines. They create safe places in a world that can often feel unsafe. They provide wisdom when we don't yet know how to ask for it. They become part of our story in ways that last for a lifetime.

I am grateful to God that Ma is still here, still herself, and still leaving an imprint on everyone who knows her. The world is a better place because of women like her, and I am a better woman because she was my neighborhood mom.

*Latonya Sterling*

# Chapter 7

# A Divine Appointment

*Honoring Mom Ruth Qualls*

Sometimes we meet people in the strangest places, in the strangest ways. Looking back, I realize those moments are often divine appointments—God's way of orchestrating connections that shape our lives forever.

In my youth, I used to walk a lot, often going far from home just to clear my mind. On one of those walks, I crossed paths with someone who would change my life. I was walking in an area not close to home when a sweet lady pulled up, rolled down her window, and offered me a ride. To this day, I don't know why I got into the car. (After all, if you watch enough movies, you know that even "sweet little ladies" can be dangerous!) But this lady was different. She was kind, genuine, and caring. What I didn't know in that moment was that this seemingly chance encounter would become one of the most significant relationships of my life. Her name is Ruth Qualls, and I affectionately call her *Mom Qualls*.

Mom Qualls ran a tutoring center that focused on teaching children the basic skills of reading and math. Education was close to her heart as a mother of two sons, both of whom excelled. When she told me about her program, I knew immediately it was something I wanted to be a part of, so I enrolled my goddaughter, Tanisha.

That decision proved to be one of the best I could have made. Not only did Tanisha benefit greatly from her tutoring, but I did too. Being around Mom exposed me to people, places, and experiences I may not have ever encountered otherwise.

Mom's tutoring center wasn't just about academics. Every year, she held special events where children were celebrated with awards, and families would gather in their best clothes to honor their accomplishments. I got to help behind the scenes, using my skills as a typesetter to create programs and materials for her events. Those experiences sharpened my abilities, expanded my confidence, and connected me with leaders in the community.

I also got to know her family. I became friends with her son Damien, who had a little crush on me, bless his heart. And I remember catching glimpses of her son Danny, who was quite attractive, though I knew I wasn't in his league back then. Still, Mom Qualls treated me like the daughter she never had, and I gladly embraced that role.

One of the most pivotal moments of my life came when I lost my job at a typesetting company. I had been falsely accused and fired, and I was furious. As I drove home, crying out to the Lord, I asked, "Lord, what am I supposed to do now?"

In that moment, I heard a voice inside say: *Go see Mrs. Qualls.* I didn't hesitate. I drove straight to her tutoring center, where she was already at work, doing what she did best. I poured out my heart, telling her what had happened and what the Lord had spoken to me. Unbeknownst to me, Mom was in the middle of training a young lady to be her assistant. Without hesitation, she looked at me and said, "I'm going to tell the other young lady that she will just be a teacher in the classroom. You will be my assistant."

Talk about confirmation! God had prepared that moment just for me. I worked with Mom for almost an entire year, and it was one of the richest learning experiences of my life. Somehow, she managed a classroom filled with children of various ages and grade levels, yet each child's needs were met. I marveled at how one woman could do what entire school systems struggle with. Mom didn't have fancy computers and tablets like schools have today. She had good old-fashioned pen, paper and index cards. Her passion for education wasn't just about children, she also believed in equipping parents to help their own children. This is her heart even today. That mindset stayed with me, shaping the way I later approached parenting and education in my own family.

Our paths intertwined again when we both ended up in the same church community. I had signed up to be an administrative assistant in the children's ministry. What I didn't realize was that Mom had been meeting with the ministry leaders before I arrived. When I walked in, she immediately began bragging about me: how great I was with kids and how much of an asset I would be to the children's ministry. Inside, I was screaming. *I didn't sign up to be a teacher! I signed up to be an administrative assistant!* But I couldn't escape her praises, and sure enough, I wound up teaching. That moment transformed me. Teaching children the Word of God stretched me, pushed me deeper into Scripture, and gave me a heart not only for academic education, but for spiritual education as well. Because of her influence, I served in children's ministry for more than twenty years.

Mom Qualls has continued to be an intricate part of my life to this very day. She has given me wisdom as a wife, wisdom as a mother, and wisdom as a believer. Her encouragement is a gift straight from the Holy Spirit. The Bible says in Romans 12:8 that encouragement (or exhortation) is a spiritual gift, and Mom has that gift in abundance.

She always speaks life into me. Her words are filled with thoughtfulness and love. Even her gifts are deeply personal. When she gives me a card, I know it is something she spent time and prayed over. She decorates them beautifully, and I hold onto them because I know they come from her heart.

Mom is also a tireless servant. She pours herself out for others, sometimes to the point of exhaustion. I fuss at her for doing too much, but her heart is always in the right place. Whether people pour back into her or not, she knows God is her strength, her tower, and her keeper. Serving is not just what she does, it is who she is.

Her love has extended beyond me to my entire family. She has poured into my husband, and she has loved my sons, Marcel and Justin, as her own grandchildren. She tutored them for a while, leaving her handprint on their lives as well. Truly, her influence has touched generations.

Yes, it was a divine appointment that day when I accepted a ride from a sweet stranger. God knew I needed a mentor, an encourager, and a spiritual mother, and He gave me Mom Qualls.

She has been a refuge, a teacher, a boss, a mentor, and a friend. More than that, she has been a vessel of God's love and wisdom in my life. The impact of her obedience, her service, and her encouragement has rippled through my marriage, my parenting, and even into the lives of my children.

Neighborhood moms are a blessing. Biological ties may define family, but spiritual bonds like these are what sustain us, shape us, and remind us of God's perfect timing. I will always be grateful that God chose to weave Mom Qualls into the story of my life.

*Latonya Sterling*

# Chapter 8

# The Prayer, The Answer, The Mom

*Honoring Mom Dolores Dotson*

One of the most extraordinary truths I have learned is this: when you ask God for what you truly *need*, He will answer—sometimes in ways that exceed your expectations. As a teenager, I became a believer, but because I didn't understand that salvation wasn't about being perfect, I thought I had failed God when I messed up. I didn't denounce Jesus, but I did denounce being a believer, believing I could no longer belong because I had done wrong. During that time, I prayed a very specific prayer: *"Lord, I don't know how to live right so I can't be saved anymore. If I ever get saved again, Lord, please send me to a ministry where I can grow. Don't let me be left hanging this time."* Years later, after rededicating my life to God as a young woman, He answered that prayer and led me to Calvary Revival Church on Little Creek Road in Norfolk, Virginia.

I began with the New Converts class, learning the foundations I had missed before. From there, I advanced into the New Members class, where I found myself praying again: *"God, please send me a woman of God who can help me as a woman. Give me someone who will walk with me, teach me, and help me grow."* I didn't ask for a program or a class—I asked for a person. And God, in His faithfulness, answered that prayer in an extraordinary way.

At the end of the New Members class, representatives from different ministries came to talk to us about areas where we could serve. Someone shared about Christian Education, saying they needed teachers and administrative assistants. Since I had experience as a secretary, administrative work sounded like an obvious choice for me. Teaching never even crossed my mind. (If you read the chapter about Mom Qualls, you'll remember how God steered me into teaching, whether I planned it or not!)

When I showed up for my ministry interview, that was the first time I met Christian Education Ministry Leaders Duncan and Dolores Dotson. Little did I know, the woman I had prayed for would be sitting across from me that day. Over time, they became Dad and Mom Dotson to me—spiritual parents who shaped my life in ways I could never have imagined.

At first, it seemed like every time Mom and I tried to connect, something would come up that pulled her away. She and Dad were hands-on leaders, constantly serving the children, the congregation, and the larger ministry. But she kept pursuing me. I vividly remember our first one-on-one conversation after service. We sat at a long table in the Christian Ed area, sitting in children's chairs. Mom was dressed in her usual black, with one of her shawls wrapped around her shoulders. As she began to speak, I instantly knew she was the answer to my prayer. At the same time, I was intimidated. She started telling me things about myself that I never shared with her. She spoke into my life with such accuracy, it shook me. How could someone I had never sat with before know this much about me? My instinct was to pull away, but her persistence drew me closer—and through her, God began to grow me.

Back then, I had plenty of issues. I had good pastors and strong teaching, but it took years for me to truly experience intimacy with God. Still, I learned invaluable lessons from Mom in those early days. I learned integrity, and I learned the importance of showing up when needed. I learned the heart of servant leadership and the value of teamwork. I also learned how to face deep-rooted issues that weren't always addressed from the pulpit. This was because Mom wasn't just a ministry leader, she was also trained in counseling. That gave her a unique depth and perspective. She didn't just see us as volunteers. She saw us as sons and daughters, people she genuinely cared for. Her ministry wasn't just about serving alongside us, but also about ensuring that we were spiritually healthy.

Her home became an extension of her ministry. Many Sundays after church, I would find myself at her house, eating at her table with other young people. Even after a long day of serving, Mom would cook, fellowship, and continue to pour into us. Those meals weren't just about food—they were about family, growth, and impartation.

Serving with Mom pushed me further than I thought I could go. I became her administrative assistant and later the leader over CIT, which prepared young people for leadership. I never saw myself in that kind of role, but being with Mom meant being stretched beyond limits.

Eventually, God called Mom and Dad Dotson back to Texas. I remember sitting in their den in Newport News when she told me the news. The thought of life and ministry without them left me breathless. I burst into tears. But God reminded me that everything He had poured into me through them was enough to sustain me. Their presence had been a gift, but ultimately, it had always been Him working through them. Because of them, I was prepared—prepared for servant leadership, prepared to be the woman God called me to be, and prepared to be a wife and a mother in the future.

After they left, I continued to grow, but I also had the joy of visiting Mom in Texas several times for a week at a time. Those visits were special because, away from the busyness of ministry, I got to have her all to myself. Mom was always busy pastoring alongside Dad, leading her women's ministry *This Is Your Season,* and traveling for missions. She is a prayer warrior and a woman who can fast like no one I know. The disciplines in Mom's life are amazing. Her compassion runs deep, and she has a gift for seeing past the surface into the heart. People who spend time in God's presence reflect it in every part of their lives, and that was true of her.

It was after her move to Texas, during one of her visits back to Virginia, that one of the most pivotal spiritual moments of my life took place. She spoke at a women's gathering held in someone's home. I remember praying silently, "Lord, I want her mantle of wisdom." I knew wisdom comes from God alone, but I longed for the careful way she used her words, her discernment in knowing when to speak and when to stay silent. That day, she placed her hand on my head as I knelt by a chair, and she prayed for me to receive the mantle of wisdom in her life. From then on, people who knew her would often tell me, "You sound just like Mom Dotson." I believe that prayer marked me forever, stirring a deep hunger for God's wisdom.

Yet, even with her depth, Mom was always relatable. She carried extraordinary humility, never boasting or putting herself above others. That humility made it even more meaningful when, during my ordination, she was invited to speak over both me and my husband. Her words were filled with wisdom, insight, and love. She spoke directly into our lives in a way that we could receive and run with, and it became a treasure we still carry. Even more, I had the privilege of hosting her in my home during that time. Having her under my roof, even briefly, felt like an honor from God Himself. For so many years she had been busy pouring herself out in ministry, so it was challenging to even get her on the phone. I never took it personally because I knew the depth of her calling, but during the time of my ordination, I had her all to myself. I didn't have to share her with the world, and I treasured every moment. That memory will remain a jewel in my heart forever.

Mom always told me the truth, even when it was uncomfortable. She challenged me to pray about decisions, pushing me to let God—not people—direct my steps. She also taught me not to let ministry demands pile up and drain me. Because of her guidance, I never experienced burnout, only healthy pause when I needed to step away for short seasons.

I really love Mom. Many amazing women have touched my life. But Mom Dotson's role in my life was distinct. Every woman God has placed in my life carries her own unique value. Each of them has taught me something vital—whether it was friendship, laughter, resilience, motherhood, or encouragement. But Mom Dotson's influence stands apart in a special way. She was not only an answer to my prayers, but also a spiritual mother who taught me how to see God differently, to grow in intimacy with Him, and to embrace servant leadership without losing myself in the process. Unlike many others who impacted me in moments or seasons, Mom's role was foundational. She challenged me when I needed to be stretched, prayed wisdom over me when I longed for more, and equipped me with discernment so that I could serve in ministry without becoming consumed or burned out. She was not just a woman who walked beside me—she was a woman who spoke into the deepest parts of my destiny.

For me, Mom Dotson is not just one of the amazing women in my story—she is the woman God used to anchor me spiritually, to prepare me for leadership, and to shape the way I minister, love, and serve. While I honor every woman who has blessed my life, I can say with certainty that the wisdom, covering, and spiritual mothering I received from Mom Dotson is unmatched. She will always hold a place in my heart that no one else can ever fill.

Young women don't be afraid to ask God for a mentor. Having a mature woman of God to walk alongside you can provide wisdom, guidance, and encouragement when life feels confusing. She can share from her own experiences and help you avoid pitfalls that she may have already overcome. A godly mentor will remind you of your identity in Christ and pray with you through challenges. Seeking out this kind of relationship is a valuable step in growing deeper in your walk with the Lord.

# Chapter 7

# Press On – My Sister, My Friend

*Honoring Lisa Evans*

In my life, I have always had friends. I never had a shortage of female companions, even if it was just one or two at a time. But it wasn't until I rededicated my life to the Lord that I connected with a woman I could truly call a sister in Christ. This was someone who was real, who was honest, who held me accountable—even when she wasn't trying to—and who pushed me beyond my limits in discovering gifts and talents God had placed inside me that I hadn't even recognized. She was and still is extremely funny, quick-witted, and unapologetically direct. You couldn't have thin skin around her because she had no filter. That great woman is my sister, Lisa Evans, who I affectionately call Boo-Boo.

When I was at CRC, Lisa and I were in the same New Converts and New Members classes. I distinctly remember, during the New Converts confirmation, watching her go around consoling others who had just received their word of affirmation. She hugged people, smiled, and encouraged them. I remember thinking to myself, *I would love to be her friend.* Later, as we went through New Members class, I didn't see her as much—after all, it was a large ministry. But toward the end, somehow, we finally connected.

At that time, I was already friends with another sister, but it wasn't a healthy friendship. We were church gossipers.

I remember one day that young lady said something negative about Lisa. Now, Lisa had already made an incredible impression on me, and she and I weren't even close yet. But when I heard those negative words, something inside me immediately shifted. I knew this wasn't a good friendship if it meant trying to separate me from the potential of having a true friend. Over time, that unhealthy friendship faded, while Lisa remained.

Eventually, Lisa and I wound up serving in the children's ministry together. I can't remember exactly how we began consistently hanging out, but I do know Lisa is incredibly artistic and gifted. She's a writer, a playwright, and a visionary. Before long, I got pulled into her projects. At the time, I was still learning typesetting skills such as designing flyers and bookmarkers, but once Lisa discovered I could do those things, she enlisted me. When Lisa enlists you, you don't really have a choice. She doesn't exactly *ask* you to help, she convinces you out of the gate, and before you know it, you're fully in the game.

So, there we were, in the game together. We spent countless late nights at her house or mine, bringing her visions to life—whether it was a play, a ministry event, or a personal project. And in between the work, we made up silly songs, cracked endless jokes, and laughed until our stomachs hurt. Sometimes we laughed so much that nothing got done, but it didn't matter. The joy of those moments made our friendship priceless.

One of the most amazing times I had with Lisa was when she and I took a trip to Busch Gardens. Lisa convinced me to get on Apollo's Chariot. I probably screamed the entire time, and when she saw my face on the picture they took during the ride, she could not stop laughing. To this day, I will not get back on Apollo's Chariot. I also remember my first women's retreat with Mom Dotson. Lisa, Meme, and I shared a room, and Lisa joked so much that I laughed and laughed. I'm sure the women in the other rooms grew tired of hearing me, but Lisa just kept stirring it up. Then she would try to act innocent, as though she hadn't done a thing. All Meme could do was laugh with us.

Lisa was always a straight shooter. If you asked her a question, she gave you the truth. Lesson learned: don't ask if you don't want to know. Her humor stung my feelings a couple of times, but never in a way that jeopardized our friendship. I recognized the jewel I had in her. I remember one ministry program where I oversaw the music. I know I cued it correctly, but somehow, when the tape was played, it was flipped the wrong way. I can't prove it, but I believe someone in the sound booth switched it on me. All I know is when the music didn't work right, Lisa gave me *that look*, the one that said everything without a word. She made some comment I can't even recall, but it was enough to make me feel like a child being scolded. I was embarrassed, standing in front of more than 300 people. But even in that moment, I knew her intention wasn't to belittle me—it was just Lisa being Lisa, and I loved her for it.

51

I also remember Lisa introducing me to a brother at the church. She didn't introduce me for romantic reasons, but as it happened, I eventually became engaged to him. Lisa, being the honest friend she was, saw right through the relationship. She could see the toxicity and advised me to walk away. Of course, I didn't listen. I had convinced myself it was the Lord's will. But my friend knew better, and she was probably praying for me the whole time. When the relationship finally ended—and only because he left me, since I wasn't wise enough to leave, Lisa was right there. She never said, "I told you so." Instead, she stood by me every step of the way, helping me through my healing process. She kept me connected, kept me laughing, and kept me moving forward when I could have easily slipped into despair.

During that season, Lisa had a phrase she repeated often: *"Press On."* Those two simple words changed my life. When I face challenges, when I feel stuck, when I don't know what to do, I still hear her voice in my head: *Press On.* It reminds me that no situation defines me, no challenge has the power to hold me down, and no struggle can separate me from the God who loves me and will never leave me. It wasn't just a phrase Lisa said. I watched her *live it.* I saw her press on through her own circumstances, and that example planted something deep in me that remains to this day.

Lisa and I are still very close. In fact, we're currently working on a project for the marriage ministry, and it feels like old times. The laughter, the late nights, the creativity, it's all still there. Lisa has always exhibited excellence in everything she does. If I had the resources, I would support anything she put her hands on. She even published a beautiful book, *From the Pages of Their Diaries,* a story about six women discovering love, identity, and forgiveness. It was so well written, and it reflects exactly who she is: a woman of vision, excellence, and heart.

Lisa was more than my maid of honor in my wedding. She was, and is, my sister, my Boo-Boo, and one of the most trustworthy, honest, and faithful friends God has ever given me.

Last year, my friend Lisa shared with me some of the things she had done—an escape room, a mystery dinner—and I knew right away that with her gifts and creativity, they had to be incredible. I asked her if she would consider bringing one of these experiences to our marriage ministry, and she gladly said yes. In September of this year (2025), she flew here from Texas to Virginia just to serve with us.

At that time, I had just come off a 10-day fast, and it seemed like everything possible was trying to interfere with this event. But God had already prepared Lisa—my press-on sister—to push through. It was a lot of planning and a lot of work, and I still can't believe how much she accomplished. She had shared with me before about a time when she prepared a mystery dinner not just in English but also in Spanish for a group larger than mine. This time, we literally had to print and create everything together to make the project happen, and once again it turned out to be excellent.

What touched me the most was her heart. Before we planned, she wanted to pray. Before the event began, she wanted to pray again. Every detail was done with excellence because she was doing it as unto the Lord. Watching her lead, seeing how smoothly it all flowed, and how the couples responded—it was clear that God was at work through her.

Lisa even took days off from her job to do this, and while she came for the mystery dinner, God also used her powerfully in my very own household. When I say that God used Lisa powerfully in my household, it was amazing watching her. The level of growth and wisdom was so astounding. Lisa has always been able to articulate things to me to help me. But this visit, I literally heard wisdom from God. She checked me in areas of my life that were quite carnal. Yet the way she checked me never came across as correction. She simply and lovingly shared the Word and wisdom without ever saying, "Tonya, you're doing this wrong," or "Tonya, you're doing that wrong." She addressed me in such a loving way that there was absolutely no way I could deny my sin or avoid dealing with it.

One of the things I have learned during a time of fasting is that listening is ministry, and her level of listening and observation was so astounding to me. I believe that while I planned for her to come here to help me with the marriage mystery dinner, God planned for her to come here to sow seeds of life—not only into me but into my entire household. I am so grateful, not only for the event, but for the way God revealed Himself through her obedience, humility, and love.

Closing out this chapter on Lisa is not easy, because her impact on my life cannot be summed up in a few sentences. But I will say this: every woman needs a Boo-Boo. Every woman needs that big sister in Christ who will push her, challenge her, keep her accountable, make her laugh until she cries, and stand by her through heartbreak and healing. A sister who is honest, who won't sugarcoat the truth, but who will never abandon you when life falls apart. Lisa has been that for me, and more. For her friendship, her laughter, her honesty, and her constant reminder to "press on," I will forever be grateful.

# Chapter *10*

# My Amazing Grace Sister

*Honoring Mikia Brigham*

Have you ever had a chance meeting with someone, only for it to flourish years later? That's exactly what happened to me and this amazing sister. While I was serving in ministry, we had what was called *care groups*. It was modeled after when Jethro told Moses in the Bible to stop trying to handle everything by himself and instead appoint others to care for the smaller matters while he dealt with the major issues. So, the ministry I attended created care groups where, instead of traditional midweek Bible study, members were divided by the area they lived in. A host home was designated, along with a care group leader.

I was supposed to be a host home, but apparently the person who signed up to be the care group leader dropped out. That left me as both the host home and the care group leader. It was a growing experience, but every now and then I wanted a break. One particular Wednesday night, after I had been leading for a couple of months, only one person showed up for the very first time—and none of my regulars came. That one person was Mikia Brigham.

Mikia is a younger sister in Christ, though I often forget that because when we talk, I feel like I'm toe-to-toe with a peer. Interestingly, she never came back to that care group again, and it would be years before our paths crossed again. After being at my former ministry for about eighteen years, my husband and I decided to leave and become part of another church. Mikia and her family were part of that ministry.

I don't specifically remember how we reconnected, but I know what tied us together was grace. Both of us were learning about the grace of God. It was refreshing to talk to someone who wasn't bound by tradition but was learning to walk away from it and embrace the love and grace of God. Grace doesn't just forgive our sin; it breaks sin's power and enables us to live free. Talking to Mikia about these things was life-giving.

From there, we started meeting for lunch monthly, or every other month. Those conversations were, and still are, amazing. They're a safe space where we can let our hair down and share openly about our marriages, our families, and the things that concern us. We speak life to one another, encourage one another, and build each other up. These are the kinds of friendships I treasure, the ones where there are no limits, because trust runs deep. I can put my heart in my sister's hands and know it's safe. If I need prayer, I know Mikia will approach our Father with sincerity and power.

I've walked with her through struggles, and it has been inspirational to see God change her heart in ways that only He could. That's Mikia—honest to the core. Her authenticity is beautiful, even in her relationship with God. She tells Him exactly how she feels and what she thinks. And if you're going to be in her life, you can expect the same honesty. If you can't handle it, you might need a different friend.

Another blessing of our relationship is that now our husbands are truly family friends. We spend quality time together, whether it's going to the farmers market, going out to eat, or fellowshipping at one another's homes. One of our yearly traditions is spending New Year's Eve with the Brighams. We used to host huge New Year's Eve parties, but after years of juggling Thanksgiving, Christmas Eve, Christmas Day, New Year's Eve, and New Year's Day, my husband and I burned out. We ended the big party, but we didn't want to stop celebrating the new year. That's when the Brighams became our annual tradition.

Mikia is fun and adventurous. She loves going out, exploring, and doing new things. You must be flexible if you want to be her friend, because she is never boring. And her sense of humor is something else—you don't see it coming, but when it hits, you're done.

One of the things I treasure most about Mikia is how we can laugh together over the smallest things. Let me share a few moments that still make me smile. Mikia and I have shared some of the funniest times together. I'll never forget the night we were at a restaurant, sitting side by side, when someone called me. Since I hadn't spoken to him in a long time, I answered to say hello and catch up. But, the conversation went on and on, and Mikia could clearly see I was trying to politely get off the phone.

In the middle of my struggle, my phone suddenly rang again. Mikia held up her phone, and to my surprise, it was my face showing on her screen. With my ignorant self, I blurted out to the man on the line, "Oh my gosh, my phone is doing something weird! I'm sitting right here next to my girlfriend, and my phone is calling her while I'm talking to you." The look on Mikia's face was priceless. The truth was, it wasn't my phone at all. It was Mikia calling me to rescue me from that never-ending conversation. I felt so crazy once I realized, but we had a good laugh about it.

The fun didn't stop there. As we pulled out of the parking lot, a guy was trying to pull in. I smiled and said kindly, "Go ahead, sweetheart, and back on up into that parking space." Mikia immediately shook her head and said, "See, I would've handled that a lot differently. I would've been like—can you wait?" I laughed and told her, "That's the balance in our friendship. I'll keep you out of jail, and you'll beat somebody up if I ever need you to." Another one of our classic moments.

And then there are the little everyday things that make our friendship special—like her riding down the street with me, scrolling through pictures of fingernails and holding them up for me to admire while I'm driving. Who else would do that?

These little moments might seem small, but they represent the joy and balance in our friendship. That's the beauty of real, genuine friendships—you can confide in one another, laugh with one another, pray with one another, and know that every moment is true and from the heart. That's exactly what I have with my grace sister, Mikia.

She has been there for me in both mountaintop and valley moments. She's come to support me when I've taught from the pulpit, even choosing to forgo services at her own ministry just to stand with me. She and her husband have joined us in fellowship for our church's marriage ministry, which meant the world to me. She was there for my ordination. When my father passed away, she played a role in his celebration of life, and I deeply appreciated her presence and support.

I've also watched her boldly step into what God asked of her. She once went on a retreat where the Lord ministered something powerful to her, and she came back and shared it with me. I knew instantly that it was a message others needed to hear, so I asked her to share it at our marriage ministry gathering. She rose to the challenge, and with grace and strength, delivered an incredible message about Abigail and how she influenced the heart of a king.

The truth is, I cannot think of a single time I needed Mikia and she wasn't there. To her, supporting me goes without saying. That's just who she is. She even calls me her "Grace Sister," and I love that. Because she is mine too— my amazing grace sister.

Friendships like the one I have with Mikia don't come along every day. They are God-ordained connections that remind you of His love in tangible form. With her, I have a safe place to be myself, a trusted sister who speaks truth in love, and a partner in the journey of grace. In a world where so many friendships are shallow or conditional, ours is rooted in something eternal: the unshakable grace of God. And for that, I will forever treasure my amazing grace sister.

# Chapter *11*

# The Queen Who Rocks and Rules

*Honoring Cathy Yarber*

There's nothing like showing up at a ministry with your children and discovering that one teacher they absolutely love. You know the teacher who shares the Word in a way that even the youngest child can understand, and who makes the teenager actually want to come back. For my daughters, that teacher was Cathy Yarber.

They loved being in her class when we were at CRC. They often told me that she knew how to reach them, and she spoke in ways they could understand. I completely understand why—because I have had the privilege of serving closely with Cathy in ministry myself. We both began at CRC and eventually found ourselves at Kingdom First, where we teamed up in youth ministry. Cathy brought the Word with creativity, always helping the kids process Scripture in practical ways.

Cathy is a woman of order. While she loves to have fun with the kids, they always knew exactly whose class they were in. She has the presence of a mother bear—if someone cross-eyed or questionable came toward her classroom, you could be sure she was on guard. When your child was in her care, your child was safe.

Beyond the classroom, Cathy is a faithful friend. I'll admit that sometimes I'm a lazy friend, too caught up in my own life to reach out. But Cathy never fails. She checks in, she shows up, and when we connect, she treats me like no time has passed at all. I like to call her a great queen because she truly rocks and rules.

Cathy is a straight shooter—no chaser. Her face tells it all. If you ask her for counsel, you will get the truth and then some. Cathy doesn't entertain foolishness, and she won't argue endlessly with you about feelings or opinions. That doesn't mean she doesn't care—it simply means she loves you enough to let you find your own way until you see God's way. In all the years I've known her, Cathy has never lived a life of compromise. While none of us are perfect, I would be hard-pressed to find some hidden sin in her closet. She is strong but also humble enough to ask for help from those she trusts. And if Cathy trusts you, you'd better not break that trust.

She's also hilarious. Cathy has an incredible sense of humor, and her facial expressions alone are worth the price of admission. I joke that she must have Puerto Rican deep down in her, because she talks with her hands, and her gestures tell a story all on their own.

Cathy is gifted in so many ways. She does her own nails, her own hair, sews, creates, and even braids hair. Some of my favorite times with her were when she used to braid my hair. Her motto is, *"I braid hair, not brain,"* meaning she doesn't braid so tightly that you can't think, like some stylists do. She always did an amazing job, and she never charged me a fortune, even though I knew her time and talent were worth far more than I could pay at the time.

Cathy can cook? Let me just say this: I used to not like quiche, but Cathy Yarber makes the best seafood quiche on this side of the world. I nearly ate a whole one by myself when she gave me two pans to take home. And her avocado rolls, wrapped like lumpia and fried to perfection, those little jokers don't survive in my house at all.

More than what she does, Cathy is remarkable for who she is. Genuine. Authentic. Caring. If she considers you family, she will always be there for you. She has been there for me. After a fire we had in 2021 I was confined to the hotel room because I was dealing with severe hip bursitis and sciatica. She massaged my leg and prayed over me. She brought me food. When my husband had heart surgery, she brought my family food. Even in her own personal struggles, she makes time for her friends. She doesn't use her trials as an excuse to withdraw. She keeps showing up, and keeps loving, keeps serving. I guess I could learn a lot from that.

Cathy Yarber is a rare gem: strong yet humble, firm yet loving, serious yet full of humor. She is faithful in friendship, fierce in protecting what matters, and fearless in her pursuit of God's way. In every way, she truly is a queen who rocks and rules. I count myself blessed to call her my sister and my friend.

# Chapter *12*

# A Bond Beyond Babysitting

*Honoring Aunt Tonya Everett*

Ever since I made the decision that I wanted to be a mom, I also decided that I wanted to be a stay-at-home mom. My desire was to give my kids my full attention once I got married. When I became an instant mom to my husband's daughters, I embraced the role wholeheartedly, but I still yearned to have a baby of my own. I thought that season would finally be my opportunity. Yet, it didn't quite work out that way. My boss didn't want to let me go, and I had trouble finding someone I could trust to watch my baby.

Enter Aunt Tonya Everett—better known simply as Aunt Tonya. She and I attended the same ministry but we didn't know each other. She was already friends with my mom. When my mom told her I was pregnant, Aunt Tonya offered herself as a sitter. Taking her up on that offer turned out to be one of the best decisions I've ever made. Though I only worked four hours a day, three days a week, little Marcel was in excellent hands. Aunt Tonya absolutely adored him.

Her role went far beyond babysitting. She and Uncle Marty quickly became friends, and before long, family. She became a trusted sister in Christ—someone I could confide in, someone who shared my love for the things of God. Picking up Marcel often turned into fellowship time in her

67

home, and soon our families were spending time together for fun and for faith. She has been present at every birthday, every milestone, every joy. When Justin was born, she loved him just as much as she did Marcel. Even when I no longer needed a sitter, she was still there, just as strong a presence in my sons' lives as she was in mine.

Aunt Tonya never hesitated to give of herself. If Marlon and I needed to travel, she was there. If we needed help on the weekend, she was there. I honestly can't recall her ever saying "no" when it came to helping with my boys. She celebrated their milestones as though they were her own, spared no expense when she wanted to bless them, and made sure they always felt her love—even slipping them gifts around Christmas, even though we don't traditionally celebrate.

She's been more than support—she's been a protector. If she even sensed that someone might try to come against me or my family, she became fierce in defense, like a pitbull. She has stood with us in ministry as well, helping us decorate and giving freely of her time. She's quirky—especially when I'm fasting and she keeps junk food on deck—but even her quirks add to the joy of knowing her. When she moved across the street, Uncle Marty joked that it was a conspiracy, but for me, it was a blessing. I could walk across the street to talk or pray, and I always knew she was lifting my family before the Lord.

And let me not forget—she is also an amazing cook. Her spaghetti is delicious, her ribs fall right off the bone, and her baked beans—especially when she sneaks in bacon just for me—are unforgettable. That joke will make her laugh when she reads this, but it's also the truth.

The story of my life as a mother would be incomplete without honoring the gift of this woman. What started as a simple babysitting arrangement turned into a lifelong bond that has shaped me, my marriage, and my children. She has stood by us in moments of joy, in seasons of transition, and in times when prayer was the greatest need. Her love has been steady, her faith has been strong, and her presence has been irreplaceable. Many children lose touch with their sitters after the early years, but my boys gained an aunt, and I gained a sister. For that, I will forever be grateful.

*Latonya Sterling*

# Chapter *13*

# Poker Face, Tender Heart

*Honoring Brenda Garcia*

I've often heard many stories of parents struggling to drop their little ones off to school for the first time, but that has never been my issue. I remember when Justin, my baby boy, was just two years old. Since Marcel was already in summer camp at his school, I decided to put Justin in as well, just so he could get acclimated to the idea of being in school. We enrolled him at Gateway Christian Academy's summer camp for two days a week. Dropping him off was no problem for me—but my husband, on the other hand, was the crybaby. That's when we met my wonderful friend Brenda Garcia. She was Justin's two-year-old teacher, and she absolutely loved her students.

After a couple of weeks, Brenda told Marlon that Justin would never truly acclimate if he only came two days a week. So, I stopped being stingy and went ahead and enrolled him for the full week.

Brenda paid close attention to every child, getting to know them individually so she could meet their specific needs. She let us know what Justin would and wouldn't eat for lunch. On days when he refused to nap, she would hold him until he fell asleep. And believe me—on days when Brenda wasn't around, I don't know who struggled more, my husband or Justin. Justin adored her. I still remember his very first art project from her class—a picture of a jar with fireflies in it. I still have that little masterpiece to this day.

I also credit Brenda with potty training my son in a very short period. By the time he entered school, he was no longer pooping on himself, though he was still wearing pull-ups. But thanks to Brenda's persistence and encouragement, he quickly learned how to stay dry, and I was very pleased. In fact, because of her training, Justin was able to enter K3 at just two years old. To this day, he remains the youngest in his class, now in eighth grade.

Brenda proved to be much more than an amazing teacher. She, along with her husband Anthony—whom we lovingly call Lil Papi—eventually became part of our family. Brenda is a straight shooter with a quick wit. She can tell a joke and keep a straight face, and you have to be careful because you don't always know if she's joking or dead serious. If you looked up the word "poker face" in the dictionary, I'm certain her picture would be there.

She has a huge, loving heart. When Brenda considers you family, there's no halfway about it. If something is going on in my life and I don't share it with her so she can help, I've broken one of her cardinal rules: *family helps family.* I've never known anyone like that before. It blesses my heart to know that, if I had no one else, I could count on Brenda to be deeply offended if I didn't let her help. That's the kind of love she carries.

Brenda is incredibly gifted. I remember when we first met, Lil Papi remodeled their kitchen. But before he could even begin, Brenda went in like a one-woman demolition crew, tearing things out so the work could get done. That's just her style—when something needs to be done, she takes the first step and then lets you catch up.

She's an amazing cook, especially of Mexican food (naturally, since she's married to a Mexican). She's also very artistic and creative. During COVID, she made masks. She creates stunning memorial blankets out of clothing from loved ones who have passed away. She bakes and decorates beautiful cakes. If you need something done and she doesn't know how, she'll figure it out, especially for those she loves.

One of the most touching things she ever did for me, beyond simply being a wonderful sister, was helping coordinate a surprise party for my fifty-fifth birthday. I am not easy to surprise, but when I came home from visiting my dad in the hospital and walked into my house, everyone shouted, *"Surprise!"* I immediately burst into tears. Brenda ran up and hugged me, and I was overwhelmed by the love and effort that went into that day.

Brenda and Lil Papi have also been a part of many of our family holiday traditions. While they may have only attended one or two of our annual Christmas Eve parties— where we invite all our extended friends and loved ones— they have been part of countless Christmas Day celebrations. Christmas Day has always been reserved for blood-related family, but in our home, anyone we call "friend" is family. Having Brenda and Lil Papi with us on those sacred days always felt right, because they are not just friends, they are family in every way.

Just as we've welcomed them into our family moments, they've included us in theirs. We celebrated Heidi's high school and college graduations with them, and we were there for Sammy's high school graduation as well. One of the greatest honors was being present for their vow renewal, a beautiful celebration of their love and commitment to one another. They've always included us in their important family events, and it has been a blessing to walk alongside each other in those milestones.

She is also a wonderful daughter to her mom. Mama is awry, but Brenda knows how to handle her with wisdom and grace. But let me say this—what you don't want to do is get on Brenda's bad side. She has a calm, quiet way of putting you in a place that you didn't even realize you needed to be in.

Brenda has shown me that sometimes the family God gives you is not the family you're born with, but the family you choose. In her, I've found loyalty, laughter, wisdom, and unconditional love. And for that, I will always be grateful.

# Chapter *14*

# My Professional Sister/Friend

*Honoring Michelle Starks*

One of the pitfalls of putting your kids in private school is that everyone is scattered. In public school, your children's classmates—and their parents—are usually right there in the neighborhood. But with private school, you often miss out on forming close relationships with other parents. Still, I had the privilege of building one very special friendship through my son Justin's time at Gateway Christian Academy.

When Justin was in K4, he met a sweet little girl named Aryele, and the two became fast friends. Their school had split into two K4 classes, and because Justin and Aryele were both the youngest in their grade, they were placed in a class with younger children rather than being placed with older K4 kids. Justin and Aryele were top students in their class and even served as marshals for the graduating kindergartners.

Somewhere in the middle of all this, I met Aryele's parents—Michelle and Grover. I don't remember the exact moment we clicked, but I believe it started with consistent conversations in the school parking lot. Eventually, those conversations turned into an invitation to our home, and the rest is history.

Michelle is unlike any of my other friends. She carries herself with such professionalism that it never fades, no matter what the setting. Don't get me wrong—she is warm, kind, loving, and an amazing wife and mother—but there's always a certain polish to the way she operates. I often joke that whenever she texts me, it feels like I'm receiving a memo from a CEO. And when she speaks, she is so articulate that there is no room for misunderstanding. If you're confused, it's not because she wasn't clear—it's because you weren't listening.

One of the blessings of our friendship was being part of a small parent prayer group at the school. Another mother had the idea for the parents of our kids' class to meet regularly, and though some came and went, me, that mother and Michelle were the ones who consistently showed up. Together, we prayed for our children, their classmates, their teachers, and the school leadership. We read Scripture and encouraged one another.

Michelle made sure my family was included in everything. Every birthday, every special event—hers, her husband's, or her children's—she always extended the invitation. She has been supportive of me as a sister and in ministry, but one day I got a taste of what makes her such a strong and honest friend. I had made the mistake of correcting her son directly without going through her. It wasn't even a major issue that I needed to address her son, but Michelle wasted no time in calling me to address it. She was absolutely right—she was sitting right there, and I should have spoken to her instead of bypassing her to correct her son. What I appreciated most was that she dealt with it quickly. Scripture says to go to your adversary quickly. Michelle wasn't my adversary, but in that same spirit, she didn't allow the enemy room to create a gap between us. She was clear, she was honest, and she was right. All I could do was humble myself, apologize, and grow from that moment. It was a valuable lesson, and it deepened my respect for her.

That's the beauty of friendship—real friends don't let you get away with things that will harm the relationship. And Michelle proved in that moment that ours was the kind of friendship where honesty and accountability would always be part of the foundation.

I think of the many fellowships we've shared at my house, especially our Christmas Eve gatherings. Michelle and Grover are such a fun couple that they were often the last to leave. Truthfully, I would sometimes kidnap them for a couple of extra hours after everyone else was gone, just to extend the laughter and the fellowship. Our children may have grown up and gone their separate ways, but our relationship remains strong. Michelle and I still fellowship as sisters, and our spouses enjoy their friendship as well.

Michelle has been a gift to me in so many ways—her professionalism, her kindness, her faith, and her honesty. She is the friend who keeps me grounded, who challenges me to grow, and who makes sure that our bond is not shallow but strong and lasting. Friendships like this remind me that God places people in our lives not just to comfort us, but to sharpen us. And for that, I am deeply grateful for the sisterhood I share with Michelle.

# Chapter *15*

# A Smile Like the Sun

*Honoring Pastor Denise Wheeler*

If you remember back in Chapter 8, I shared about my mentor, Mom Dotson. She was the woman I had prayed for to help me grow, and God answered. But after Mom and Dad Dotson moved back to Texas, I felt alone. I had amazing friends, but I deeply missed having a mentor. I could still call her here and there, but when Mom became heavily involved in missions, it was almost impossible to have her for long periods of time.

I remember one of the mothers in the church saying to me, *"Now that she's gone, you've got to grow up and learn how to walk on your own—just you and Jesus."* I took that to heart. I understood what she meant, and I embraced the truth of it. Still, there was a part of me that longed for that spiritual mother figure I had lost.

A close friend of ours had invited a couple to our house for a fellowship. He told me they were pastors. When they first came to our home and I met them for the first time, I was struck immediately by their humility. They didn't show up as "titles." They came into our home as everyday people who laughed, fellowshipped, and genuinely cared. They were Pastors James and Denise Wheeler.

One day, after venting on Facebook about things that frustrated me in the church, God answered that cry in an unexpected way. Pastor James saw my post. Instead of addressing me out in the open, he wisely chose to DM me. In doing so, he heard my heart's cry. God allowed him to see beyond my frustration and recognize that I didn't need another mentor—I needed a safe place to keep growing. Not a place of pressure, not a place of pretense, but a place where I could simply continue becoming who God had called me to be.

Without us even being part of their ministry, they invited us to their home for dinner and spent quality time with us. Pastor James talked a lot, but Pastor Denise was a quiet listener. They were kingdom-minded—if you're part of the Body of Christ, you're family. And with them, we felt that. They looked after my husband and me when he had to undergo gallbladder surgery. That spoke volumes about who they were.

So, when the time came for us to leave our previous ministry, it was easy to transition into theirs. It wasn't that the ministry we left was bad ... not at all. It was simply time to move forward. That decision was later confirmed when the ministry dissolved because God had called our pastor into a new assignment.

When my husband and I first arrived at the Wheelers' ministry, we enjoyed it right away. Within about three months, I began serving. A friend of mine kept saying, *"You're supposed to be close to Denise."* At the time, I couldn't see it. She was kind, and I respected her, but I felt a little on the outside. The women in the ministry seemed to already have a close-knit bond, and my own insecurities made me question whether there was a place for me among them.

Then I started to settle in, becoming comfortable with everyone and everything. That's when something inside me sprang up—discontentment, complaining, grumbling, pride, and self-righteousness. With that storm swirling inside of me, I began to position my heart toward leaving. I became super critical of everything and everyone. When I reached the point of wanting to walk away, the Lord spoke gently: *"Stay."*

It took me a while to see it, but I realized the enemy was trying to use my weaknesses to keep me from recognizing something vital: Pastor Denise was meant to be a very important part of my life. Once I understood that, I began to fight. I prayed and allowed God to deal with my mindset, my heart, and my perspective. And the more God worked in me, the more clearly I began to see her.

What I saw was a woman who is kind, loving, and radiant. She has a smile so bright it feels like God took the sun out of the sky and placed it on her face. When she hugs me, it blesses my heart—it's never the stiff, religious pat on the back, but a real embrace. Even when I don't fully agree with her, it doesn't change how I feel about her, because God transformed my heart to see the beauty of who she is. Pastor Denise is a prayer warrior and a passionate worshiper. She loves God deeply, and her greatest desire is to see people know Him for themselves—to experience the beauty of worship, the privilege of His presence. She may sometimes come across as fussing, but what she's really saying is, *"I love you, and I want the best for your life and your walk with God."*

She has a way of drawing things out of people. She'll ask you to do something and give you the choice to say yes or no—but I believe she asks because she already sees it in you. Your yes isn't really to her; it's a response to God saying, *"This is what I put in you. Bring it out."*

She is a true servant leader. She never asks anyone to do what she won't do herself. From cleaning bathrooms to serving in the kitchen to shampooing carpets, she's all in. She constantly teaches about using the gifts God has placed inside of us, gifts we too often sit on. Many times I've heard her say, *"Some of you in here have books in you."* For years, I dismissed it, thinking she was talking to others. But then came my first book, *The Beginning of My Beginning.* From there, God poured out more books through me.

When I finally handed her that first book, it was nerve-racking—but God knew what He was doing. She became my accountability. She pointed out things I needed to change so that I wouldn't risk damaging anyone with my words. I thank God for that correction, because unchecked, I could have caused harm. Once I got past the initial shock of sharing, it became easier to hand her my second book.

Leaders like Pastor Denise are a blessing to the Body—they bring order, beauty, and honor to God's house. There have been times when I didn't agree with something she said, only to later realize how valuable her words were.

My pastors never force us to attend events, but they always encourage us to support one another. Sometimes I don't feel like doing it, and I don't. But I'll never forget the first time I was invited to speak at an anniversary service for another ministry. I was shocked and nervous, but as I stood in the pulpit, I looked out and saw Pastor Denise's smile. It was the smile of a mother, and it gave me the confidence to stand and deliver. Ultimately, it was the Holy Spirit working through me, but I know God also worked through her smile in that moment.

What has meant so much to me as well is the way she has been there for my family. She was there for my mother when my father was ill, and again when he passed away. She was there when my mom lost her brother. My mother doesn't even attend our ministry, but because she is an extension of me—and of the kingdom family—Pastor Denise showed up for her. That's above and beyond what I've ever seen.

In some ways, I can see glimpses of similarities of Mom Dotson in her. I've never looked at Pastor Denise as a mother figure; to me, she feels more like a big sister with the same warmth and love. Yet, there was one moment at the altar when she prayed for me and called me *daughter,* and I felt it deep in my soul. It made me smile even afterward, because it was another reminder of God's hand in connecting me to her. She isn't a replacement for Mom Dotson—she is uniquely herself. And that is exactly what I need.

God knew what He was doing when He led me to Word & Worship Center. Even if I hadn't prayed for it, I believe He orchestrated it. Pastor Denise Wheeler is not just a pastor to me—she is a sister, a leader, a guide, and a radiant light whose smile and presence reflect the heart of God. She has challenged me, encouraged me, corrected me, and celebrated me. She has helped shape me as a servant, as a writer, as a minister, and as a daughter of the King.

I have heard people say she is tough or stern. But, I don't see her that way. She is simply very passionate about her desire to see people grow in their relationship with Father. I see that she carries her own unique grace that God knew I would need for this season of my life. For that, I will always honor her and thank God for placing her in my journey.

# Chapter *16*

# Unique Elegance Unique Ministry

*Honoring Kanisha Johnson*

You just never know where you're going to meet the right people, but somehow God has a way of connecting you with them in the simplest arenas of life. I am the type of person who cannot stand sitting in the average salon. Historically, salons were places where crazy stuff was playing on the TV, loud music filled the room, women were gossiping, and some man would come in selling bootleg DVDs or CDs. I was very grateful when they introduced salon malls—indoor strips where each stylist has their own private booth with a door that closes, separating them from all the others.

Unfortunately, my longtime stylist passed away, so I was left to fend for myself and pretty much struggle with my own hair for years. That changed the day my sister walked into church with her hair looking absolutely fly. When I asked her who had done it, she sent me to a salon called *Unique Elegance.* "Unique" was an understatement.

The owner was Kanisha Johnson, and to call her just a hairstylist would not do her justice. Little did I know that sitting in Kanisha's chair would literally shift my mindset about my future. Kanisha is the kind of stylist who doesn't just do hair—she does people. What I mean is, she sees beyond the crown on your head and perceives the needs of your heart. When you sit in her chair, you don't just get top-notch hair care—you get ministered to. From the very beginning, Kanisha spoke to me as if she had known me for years. She spoke life into me and encouraged me exactly where I needed it most.

I've always been the one to encourage others, to speak life into them, but here I was with someone who barely knew me pouring into me as though we had a history together. I didn't just leave her chair with a beautiful hairstyle—I left with a lifted, encouraged heart. I had to come back. And every time I returned, she poured into me again. She didn't tiptoe around what I did or didn't believe. She simply and boldly declared whatever the Lord gave her to say.

Kanisha is a very transparent person, but she doesn't trust her heart with just anyone. That's why it was a privilege when she would open up to me, sharing pieces of her own journey. In the beginning, she would say things that were way over my head, and at times I thought they were a little "out there." But over time, the Lord began to chip away at the wall I had built, the one that made it hard for me to fully receive the counsel I needed to move forward in the areas where He was calling me.

Kanisha was determined to help me see who I was and what God wanted to do in and through me. She was adamant about pushing me past my comfort zone. If I'm honest, while my flesh loves attention, a part of me has always wanted to slip quietly into obscurity, unseen and unknown, because I dislike responsibility. But Kanisha would not let me hide. She pushed me—not harshly, but persistently—until I began to embrace the truth of who I was in Christ.

Because of her persistence in speaking life over me, I eventually stepped into my future. When I allowed my pastors to ordain me as a minister, it wasn't about receiving a title; it was about being positioned for access. I'll never forget watching the video of my ordination and seeing the moment when my pastor called all the pastors and ministers to the front, no matter what ministry they belonged to. In that video, I saw Kanisha standing beside me. It blessed my heart because she was in her rightful place. She had been a major part of the process of God bringing me to that moment, and it was my privilege to have her there as much as it was her privilege to be part of it.

Kanisha has been like iron sharpening iron in my life. When I look at her shop, I don't see a simple salon. I see a unique place of ministry—a fellowship space where women gather to encourage one another, build one another, and learn from one another. I've watched her go through struggles, but I've also had the privilege of witnessing the amazing work of the Lord in her life.

Every time I sit in her chair, it feels like a gift. Every time I schedule an appointment, I know I will walk away with more than a nice hairdo. I leave with a renewed spirit, an uplifted heart, and the reminder that God connects us with certain people for reasons far greater than we realize.

Kanisha has shown me that God can place ministry in the most unexpected spaces—even in a salon chair. She is proof that obedience to God's voice can transform ordinary work into extraordinary impact. My life is richer because of her words, her faith, and her relentless push to help me step into all that God called me to be. She will always remain one of the unique treasures in my journey, and I am forever grateful for her.

# Chapter *17*

# Finding Treasure in the Fire

*Honoring Lakisha Treasure*

Sometimes in life, we go through things that are very difficult. Sometimes we contribute to the issue, and other times circumstances happen beyond our control. Either way, God can use it for His glory. Back in August 2021, my family had a house fire that left us displaced. It seemed like an uphill battle with the insurance company until we eventually realized the problem wasn't entirely the insurance company, it was that we didn't have the right team.

I reached a breaking point where I cried out to God: *"Lord, we need You to bring someone who can put our house back together with the little money we have, because we can't do this on our own."* After months on this roller coaster of uncertainty, the insurance company finally gave us the final check. With the check in hand, we still didn't know what to do. Again, I cried out to God: *"Lord, we're not going to do anything. We're not going to look for a contractor. We need You to bring the right person to us."*

Every year our neighborhood holds a block party. We had never gone before. The summer of 2023, our wonderful neighbor Irene, who lived behind us, convinced my husband to come to the block party—even though we still weren't back in our house. So, my husband went, and the entire family followed. While I was standing and talking with one of the ladies in the neighborhood, a beautiful young woman walked up. The lady I was talking to introduced us, and her name was Lakisha Treasure. We call her Kisha—and she truly is a treasure.

As we began to share information, I told her we lived in the house on the street with all the storage pods in the driveway because of the fire. Amazingly, she said that she and her husband often walked past our house, wondering what had happened. They thought maybe we were military or living out of town. But that day, she got her answer.

I explained some of the issues we were having with finding a contractor who would work with the limited funds we had. Without hesitation, she said, "We can help you." She began to tell me about her husband Damion, who was incredibly skilled at remodeling homes. He had literally transformed their house with his own hands. That day marked the beginning of a beautiful friendship that still exists today.

Kisha has a distinctively angelic personality. She is sweet, intuitive, and humble. She radiates the love of God and always speaks well of others. She is an amazing wife, a devoted mother, and a dynamic entrepreneur. If I had known her in my younger years, I probably would have been running a conglomerate by now—because she's the kind of woman who pulls you along and makes you believe you can do anything. Her husband can attest to that.

Kisha is absolutely glamorous. I am not exaggerating—she looks good in everything. She has the most beautiful smile, a heart of gold, and a quiet but undeniable strength that reflects her love for God. When I listen to her talk and watch how she carries herself with her husband and children, I see how deeply she supports her family with grace and consistency.

Even though we haven't known each other all our lives, she has been such a support to me. On September 1, 2024, when I was ordained, she was there. Seeing her face in the crowd blessed my heart, and I knew it was an honor for her to share that moment with me. When my father passed away in May 2025, she came to his celebration of life. Again, it touched my heart that she showed up—not because I asked her, but because she cared.

We don't hang out all the time. We don't talk on the phone every day. We usually just see each other around the neighborhood. Sometimes our sons spend time together, or she'll knock on my door, or I'll knock on hers. It's not a relationship I can neatly define. It's both simple and profound, distant yet close. But it matters. And she matters.

Kisha is more than just a neighbor. She is a gift from God, a living answer to prayer, and a reminder that sometimes God plants treasures right where you live.

*Latonya Sterling*

# Chapter *18*

# The Hidden Jewel

There are some friendships that shine in plain sight, and there are others that are hidden—like a jewel kept safe and out of view, but no less valuable. This chapter is about one such friendship, a woman whose name I cannot share, but whose impact on my life is undeniable.

I met her through ministry. We weren't serving together, but someone else in the ministry felt she needed a godly friend and connected us. When I first encountered her, I realize now that I was immature. I didn't yet know how to walk alongside someone without becoming so immersed in their issues that I let them affect me. I desperately wanted to help her in every way I could, but my self-righteousness got in the way. I tried to fix things that were never mine to fix. And because I couldn't handle the weight of her struggles, it wore me down emotionally.

There came a season when we stopped communicating. At the time, it felt like loss. But looking back, I see God's hand in it. In that quiet season, He began to work on me. He taught me how to be stronger, steadier, less easily swayed by other people's emotions. He taught me how to care deeply without internalizing everything. And so, when she came back into my life, I was better equipped to be her friend without trying to play God in her life.

From her, I learned so much. I learned how to be a mother to my daughters, not a drill sergeant. I learned the value of gentleness in a home. Because she had walked through the experience of a previous marriage, she often gave me godly insight into my own relationship with my husband. She was also a student of the Word. Whenever she learned something new and shared it with me, it pushed me to dig deeper in my own study of Scripture. I used to tell her that I wanted to ride her coattails—because while she didn't see herself as doing anything great, I could see God moving in her life, and I wanted to be right there, holding on.

Our friendship has not been without its challenges. There have been misunderstandings, words spoken that didn't need to be spoken, and times when repentance and forgiveness were necessary. There were seasons of separation, but each time we reconnected, I found myself stronger, more mature, less easily offended. Things that once bothered me no longer had power over me. I no longer felt the need to be "enough" for her, because God reminded me that it was never my role to fix her life. My call was to simply be her friend, to show up, to love, and to let Him do the work only He could do.

Still, there were times I unintentionally hurt her, and she needed space. I learned to give her that space, always ready and willing to receive her back when she felt comfortable. That is one of the hardest things about friendship—stepping back when you want to be close, staying quiet when you want to speak, waiting when you want to act. But I learned through her that love sometimes looks like patience, and friendship sometimes means giving room instead of holding tight.

We haven't spoken in a while, but there was no way I could write this book without writing about her. Whether she realizes it or not, she has been a tremendous part of my spiritual growth and of my understanding of what it means to love as a friend. She taught me how to hang in there when life and circumstances try to pull people apart. She showed me what it means to keep coming back, to forgive, to rebuild.

If she were to call me today, I would answer without hesitation. I would be there as if nothing had ever happened, because I value her that much. I value our relationship that much. This friendship may not always look neat or easy, but it is a jewel—precious, rare, and unforgettable.

*Latonya Sterling*

# Chapter *19*

# A Circle of Many Crowns

*Honoring the Tapestry of Sisters*

There are more wonderful women in my life than I could ever capture in a single book. Each one has left her imprint on me, and together they form a circle of influence, encouragement, and love that has carried me through many seasons. This chapter is like a quilt—stitched together with the influence of so many women who shaped me. It is dedicated to those whose names may not fill entire chapters on their own, but whose presence in my life has been priceless.

I'll begin with my goddaughter, Tanisha Bolden. When I was younger, I was extremely selfish, and the thought of having children never crossed my mind. My plan was to work in corporate America, marry a corporate man who didn't want kids either, and build a comfortable life. But when one of my close childhood friends, Annette, had a beautiful little girl and asked me to be her godmother, everything changed. Becoming her godmother planted a seed in me that I didn't even realize would grow. Her mother, Annette, was a very close friend in my youth. We hung out and did many fun things together. We also had a mutual friend named Petrina, whom God used to lead me to a corner church where I first heard the Gospel and became a born-again believer.

Years later, I married a man with four daughters and a son, and suddenly my life was full of children. Tanisha's presence was a turning point, the first patch in the quilt that prepared my heart for motherhood in ways I could never have planned.

I also think back to the wonderful women who stood beside me at my wedding. They were sisters I served closely with in Christian Education at a previous ministry— Stephanie Iverson, Rosetta Jones, and Karen Calbourne (who has since passed on). The four of us were tightly knit in ministry, and their loyalty extended into my personal life. Stephanie, though the church had already assigned a wedding director, became my personal director because I trusted her so much with the details that mattered most. Rosetta and Karen stood as greeters, welcoming people on that special day. Having attended other weddings and hearing the horror stories of brides forcing their attendants to spend hundreds on dresses, I was determined not to burden my friends. I told them simply to wear something close to my colors. But these incredible women did more than that—they went to the same shop where I purchased my gown and bought matching dresses of their own. When I went to pay for my bridesmaids' gowns and shoes, the cashier told me there were additional items on my account that had already been paid for. Because they had joined my wedding party order, they had received a discount. The only thing unpaid were their shoes, which I gladly covered. It humbled me deeply that they had sacrificed financially when

I had asked nothing of them, simply because they wanted to make my day extra special. Their generosity was another bright square stitched into my quilt of friendships.

Another unforgettable blessing in my life was my roommate, Adrienne Petty. I've heard the horror stories about female roommates and the conflicts that often arise, but my story is quite the opposite. Adrienne and I lived together for nearly three years, and not once did we have an argument or even a serious disagreement. She was easy to live with, and we respected each other's space. When Adrienne wanted company, she was fun and engaging; when she needed solitude, I gave her that space without offense. She had a quiet strength and a thoughtful way of carrying herself that made our home peaceful. Living with Adrienne was one of the smoothest, most enjoyable experiences of my young adult life, and I have always been grateful for that season before marriage. She represented the steady stitching that held me together at a time when I was still learning who I was.

Today, I think about the women I serve with at Word & Worship Center, each of whom brings something beautiful to our ministry family. Jackie Downs is the definition of a servant. If you were to look up the word *servant* in the dictionary, her picture would be there. She faithfully supports our pastors and, if anyone else needs her, she shows up without complaint, giving her all. She is an incredible grandmother, she was a loving wife, and the kind of person you want on your team in any arena. Jackie has walked through many trials, but her faith in God has remained steadfast. She never lets her struggles stop her from serving, and if she has a personal need, you would need the jaws of life to pull it out of her. Jackie's faithfulness is like the strong binding that holds the quilt's edges together.

Then there is Helen, another wonderful servant. When she arrives at an event, she doesn't wait to be asked—she simply finds what needs to be done and does it. She is always smiling, always willing. I admire the way she and her husband faithfully bring their trail of grandchildren to church. Her desire is to leave a legacy of faith so that every one of her grandchildren knows that Jesus is Lord. Helen adds warmth to the quilt, the kind of stitching that keeps future generations covered.

Our ministry also has Olivia, the Songbird. Her voice is strong and beautiful, but it's her character that leaves the greatest impression. Olivia is humble, gentle, and wise. She has the gift of discernment, knowing when to speak and when to remain silent, and when she does speak, her words carry weight. She is caring, loving, and sharp in her appearance, always dressed with style. When Olivia teaches, it is like thunder rolling—quiet power that makes you stop and listen. Olivia is the thread of wisdom running through the fabric, holding things steady.

And then there is Jacquella, in a class all by herself. She is one of the most articulate women I have ever met. I love to hear her teach and speak because she always says exactly what she means and means exactly what she says. She

100

is gracious, fair, and nonjudgmental, always giving people a chance to be heard. She is a faithful wife who always speaks highly of her husband and ensures he is seen for who he truly is, not lumped into stereotypes. Quella is the helpmeet that encourages her husband to be the best that he can be, and she trust God to do in him whatever needs to be done. She covers her husband in prayer and is wise about who she divulges any information to regarding him. She is the epitome of the woman who "covers her head." She is also her own woman, creative and unique in style, often changing her hair in bold, beautiful ways. But what I admire most about her is her gift of encouragement. She uplifts everyone she encounters, pouring into her five children with patience and love, teaching them discipline, self-awareness, and assertiveness. Managing five different personalities with such grace is no small task, yet she does it with remarkable strength. Jacquella's encouragement is like a bright patch in the quilt that catches your eye and makes you smile.

Elder Tonyia Finnie is another jewel. She may be small in stature, but she carries the bite of a Chihuahua when it comes to the Word of God. She doesn't tolerate foolishness, and she knows the Word well enough to shut down anything contrary. She is fun, but she also demands respect for her boundaries. I value her because she is real, she tells the truth, holds you accountable, and doesn't sugarcoat. She has faced many challenges, but by God's grace, she has always bounced back. She is also a devoted wife, and it is beautiful to watch the love and respect she shares with her husband. Tonyia adds bold colors to the quilt—fiery shades that remind you strength and truth are beautiful, too.

Then there is Talia, the quiet sweet spirit of our ministry. She sings on the praise and worship team with a soft yet beautiful voice. She is gentle and approachable, and you can clearly see her attentiveness as a mother reflected in the sweet personalities of her daughters. Raising three girls at once requires wisdom and intentionality, and I can tell she pours into each of them individually, shaping them into young women of grace and strength. Talia is like the soft fabric of the quilt—subtle, but essential, bringing comfort and sweetness to the whole design.

Finally, I cannot fail to honor Mother Bea, a powerhouse in prayer. If we could see into the spiritual realm, I believe we would witness demons scattering when she begins to pray. She is full of wisdom, but she carries it humbly, waiting for God's timing to speak. She doesn't rush to offer her opinion, but when the Spirit of God stirs her, her words carry weight. She is a mother to the ministry, always providing something for the children, always encouraging, always seeing the best in people. She is also deeply thoughtful sending out cards that uplift and periodically texting us in the ministry with words of life right when we need them. It is a rare and beautiful gift to be the well-respected mother of a ministry, the one whose presence brings comfort, whose prayers bring strength, and whose love quietly but powerfully holds the family of God together.

Mother Bea's prayers are like the strong, hidden stitches that hold everything together, even when you can't see them.

I'm certain there are many more women I could mention, because I have never had a shortage of godly women in my life. Each one has impacted me in unique ways. Together, they form a circle of many crowns, and like a quilt, each piece is stitched together to cover me with love, strength, wisdom, and grace. And for that, I am profoundly grateful.

# Chapter 20

# My Silent Cheerleader

*Honoring Grandma Mary Arrington*

Some encounters in life may seem brief, but their impact ripples for years. That is how it was with Grandma. I just recently learned her real name. We all simply called her "Grandma." I only met her once, but in that single meeting, I could tell she was a woman gifted by God, carrying a prophetic grace that seemed both gentle and powerful. She asked me to come back alone another time, without the friend who brought me, but I never did. I didn't realize then how much that decision would weigh on me later.

During our meeting, she asked how I was doing, and with the excitement of youth, I showed her my beautiful engagement ring. She looked at it, smiled faintly, and let out a quiet laugh under her breath. At the time, I didn't understand it, but later my friend told me Grandma already knew I would not end up marrying the man who gave me that ring. And she was right. Grandma had an insight that saw beyond the surface—into the truth of what was and what would be.

Though I never went back to see her, Grandma was still working behind the scenes on my behalf. She stayed in touch with my friend, asking for updates about me, giving wise, godly counsel on how to deal with me, guide me, and help me grow. At the time, I thought everything came directly from my friend, but later I learned that Grandma was the wellspring behind much of that counsel. My friend, weary of my selfish and self-centered ways in those years, might have walked away if not for Grandma's encouragement. Yet Grandma's faith in what God would do in me never wavered.

Her confidence in God's work in me was so strong that when she was to receive an award, she told my friend to have me accept it on her behalf. My friend asked what she wanted me to say, and Grandma simply replied that I would know. I don't remember exactly what words I spoke, but I do know this: I emphasized that the award meant nothing compared to living a life that honored God. When my friend relayed my words back to Grandma, she said, "That's exactly what I would've said." That moment confirmed just how much God had been quietly stitching our lives together through her obedience.

My one regret is that I never returned to sit with Grandma again. But even so, her fingerprints are all over my journey. She spoke into my future through my friend— telling me I would one day run a business, serve in ministry, and even write books. At the time, I laughed at every single one of those declarations. Yet here I stand today, living out each word she spoke by the Spirit of the Lord.

Grandma's story reminds me of Jesus' words in Matthew 6:6: *"Your Father, who sees what is done in secret, will reward you."* She was the very picture of that scripture— working in secret, praying in secret, encouraging in secret—

and God honored her faithfulness. Though I didn't know the full extent of her investment in me until later, I see now how God used her hidden labor of love to help shape my destiny.

Grandma may have only touched my life once in person, but she touched it many times in spirit. Her unseen prayers, her prophetic words passed down through my friend, and her unwavering confidence in God's plan for me shaped my future in ways I didn't realize until years later. I take comfort in knowing that even though we never had that second meeting, she still played her part faithfully. She was, and always will be, *my silent cheerleader*—the one working quietly in the background, believing in God's work in me when I didn't believe in myself. And one day, when I leave this world, I will see her again—not for counsel or correction, but for rejoicing. That will be the meeting we never had on earth but will treasure in eternity.

# Conclusion
# The Tapestry of Sisterhood

As I bring this book to a close, I am in awe of the tapestry of women God has woven into my life. Each one has left her unique fingerprint on my heart—mentors, sisters, friends, neighbors, teachers, encouragers, prayer warriors, and even those silent cheerleaders working in the background when I didn't know I needed them. Together, their lives and their love have shaped me into the woman I am today.

Looking back, I see that some relationships were born out of prayer, like Kisha or Mom Dotson, whom I specifically asked God for. Others came by "chance" meetings that turned out to be divine appointments, like Mom Qualls or Kanisha in the salon chair. Some grew from shared ministry, like Cathy and the Word and Worship women. Some from family ties, like my Mom and my sister Gina. There are people cheering for me behind the scenes such as Grandma. Some even came wrapped in challenges, like Michelle, who sharpened me with honesty when I needed it most. And then there are those friendships that go through seasons of silence but still leave undeniable impact.

If there is one thing these stories teach us, it's that God is intentional. He knows who we need and when we need them. He knows how to pair personalities, sharpen weaknesses, and bring encouragement at just the right time.

He knows how to give us friends who will laugh with us, cry with us, correct us, and cheer for us.

Too often, we as women tell ourselves that close, meaningful friendships are too hard or too messy. We may carry scars from betrayal or disappointment, and sometimes we let those wounds keep us from trying again. But my prayer for you is that you won't stop seeking. Good women friendships are out there. They may not always look like you expect, but they are worth finding.

I challenge you to **be open, be prayerful, and be courageous.** Ask God to send the right women into your life and trust Him when He does. Be willing to let others see the real you. Be willing to love, to serve, to forgive, and to grow. And don't be afraid of correction or challenge, that's often where the richest growth comes from.

Sisterhood is not about perfection; it's about presence. It's about walking with one another through the joys and the storms, lifting each other up, and pointing each other back to Jesus when the road gets rough. It's about being iron that sharpens iron, love that never gives up, and grace that keeps showing up.

So, treasure the women God has already placed in your life. Nurture those relationships. And keep your heart open for the divine appointments yet to come. Because somewhere out there is another woman waiting to be your sister, your encourager, your prayer partner, your safe place, your laughter in the midnight hour. And somewhere out there, you may be that woman for someone else.

Beautiful bonds don't just happen—they're built. And when they're built on Christ, they will last a lifetime and beyond.

## Reflection Prayer

Father, I thank You for every woman You've placed in my life—those who have mentored me, challenged me, encouraged me, and walked beside me. Thank You for divine appointments and for friendships that reflect Your love. Teach me to treasure these bonds and to nurture them with grace and humility. Help me to also be that kind of woman for others—an encourager, a truth-teller, a safe place, and a sister in Christ. May every friendship I build bring glory to You and remind the world of the beauty of Your family. Amen.

*Latonya Sterling*

# Previous Works by
# Latonya LSimmons Sterling

The Beginning of My Beginning
Freedom: From Religious Rituals to Intimacy with God

Explore the journey from religious bondage to a personal, transformative relationship with God. This book invites readers into a deeper intimacy with God, embracing freedom through grace and love.

God is Love: More Than a Feeling

A journey of discovering what real love is and learning how God's love empowers you to live and function in every area of life.

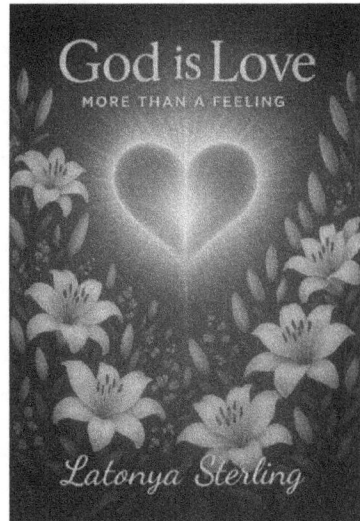

# COMING SOON

Til Death Do Us Part
Understanding and Keeping Your Wedding Vows

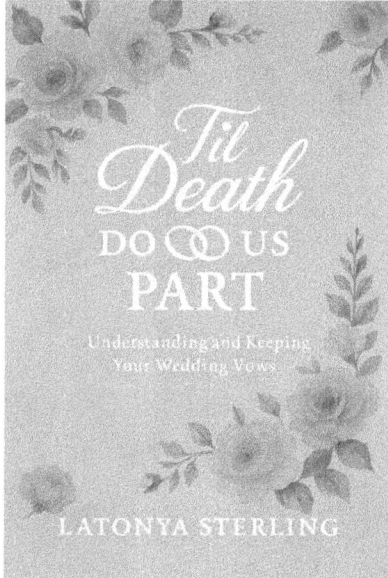

Marriage is more than a one-day ceremony. It's a covenant. This book unpacks the vows we speak at the altar and shows what it means to live them out daily. It's not a book of judgment, but encouragement, hope and truth. Whether newly married, seasoned or preparing for the journey, all couples need to be inspired to see the marriage vows as a lasting promise, not just words.

www.ingramcontent.com/pod-product-compliance
Lightning Source LLC
Chambersburg PA
CBHW072234290326
41934CB00008BA/1283